ECHOING THE WORD

ECHOING THE WORD

The Bible in the Eucharist

PAULA GOODER
and
MICHAEL PERHAM

First published in Great Britain in 2013

Society for Promoting Christian Knowledge
36 Causton Street
London SW1P 4ST
www.spckpublishing.co.uk

British Library Cataloguing-in-Publication Data
A catalogue record for this book is available from the British Library

ISBN 978-0-281-06913-2
eBook ISBN 978-0-281-06914-9

Typeset by Graphicraft Limited, Hong Kong
First printed in Great Britain by Ashford Colour Press
Subsequently digitally printed in Great Britain

eBook by Graphicraft Limited, Hong Kong

Produced on paper from sustainable forests

For
Vivienne Faull and Rosemary Lain-Priestley
with thanks

Contents

Acknowledgements

Michael Perham worked with other Church of England liturgists to develop the *Common Worship* services, including the Eucharist. He readily and gratefully acknowledges that some of the historical background to these texts is drawn from *Companion to Common Worship* (SPCK, 2001), to which he was himself a contributor, and which was edited by Paul Bradshaw.

Introduction

There must be very few Christians who do not acknowledge the importance of the Bible in worship. At the very least they will read the Scriptures, often under the discipline of a lectionary that ensures they read a wide and balanced selection. They may also sing the Scriptures in biblical canticles or in songs that stay very close to biblical texts. If they follow a set liturgy, as Anglicans among others do, they will be aware that their Morning and Evening Prayer is strongly biblical, for, as well as readings from the Scriptures, there are psalms, responsories and canticles lifted straight from the pages of the Bible.

But what of the Eucharist? The Bible readings are there, of course, with the proclamation of the Gospel reading as something of a climax to the liturgy of the word, but is the Eucharist a biblical service? In *Echoing the Word* a biblical scholar and a liturgist set out to explore that question together, doing it principally in relation to the current liturgy of the Church of England, *Common Worship* Order One. But our hope is that this will not prove to be a book only for English Anglicans but will be helpful to other Christians, both because we have a great many of the eucharistic texts in common and because what emerges, as much as fascinating insights into particular texts, are some principles with which those who fashion our liturgies work.

What we discover is that there is hardly a sentence in the eucharistic liturgy that does not echo the Scriptures. Sometimes we find whole sentences of the Bible knitted into a prayer or some other text. Sometimes we find words and phrases skilfully incorporated in a way that respects their meaning in their original context. At other times we find that those words and phrases, lifted from that context, are being used in ways that would be a huge surprise to their original authors. And just sometimes there is an allusion to a well-known biblical passage, without any quotation from it at all, but with language that puts us in mind of a whole story even though it isn't told. It simply jogs our memory to bring to our mind something deeply familiar to us from reading the Bible. In *Echoing the Word* we explore biblical resonances in the texts in relation to nearly all the liturgical texts. (We have not looked at the creed which, though it has its place in the liturgy, is a different kind of text and would need a book of its own. Indeed it has had many books of its own!)

Very few contemporary liturgical texts have been created by men and women sitting down at a desk with nothing open in front of them but a Bible. Even that great Anglican liturgist, Thomas Cranmer, at the time of the Reformation, didn't work like that. Nearly always the liturgists will also have before them some of the texts that have come down the centuries and gone through many revisions and changes to fit them for new purpose and changing culture. And more important than the texts that they spread around them as they work is what they carry in their memory, not only of biblical material but also of the whole praying life of the Church. Some of it they carry un-consciously. Sometimes they can believe they are being creative when all they are really doing is calling to mind something lodged deep inside them from years of prayer and worship.

So to explore a text we need first to establish its story. How do we come to have it in our liturgy? Sometimes the history of a text takes us back to church life as early as the second century. Quite often in Anglicanism it takes us back to the sixteenth century and the first liturgies in English. But there are other occasions when we can go back only a few years to a period of unparalleled liturgical creativity in the Church of England, as in other Western churches, in the final decades of the last century. Whatever the case, the story needs to be told.

The Church of England since the Reformation in the sixteenth century has ordered its liturgy in a distinctive way. This liturgical provision has not only shaped the worship of the Church of England but has also influenced Anglican worship across the world. As so often, influence is a two-way street and more recently the Church of England has received texts back from the resources of Anglican provinces in the worldwide communion.

Though consciously distinctive, Anglican worship is a product of the context from which it emerged. In the sixteenth century, the liturgy emerged from the worship of the medieval Church, and in fact still retains much in common with the liturgical provision of the Roman Catholic Church (both its traditional liturgy and its twentieth-century reforms), as well as, at the time of the Reformation, drawing also on the work of the sixteenth-century continental reformers, including Martin Luther (1483–1546), Ulrich Zwingli (1484–1531) and John Calvin (1509–64). There have been two highly creative periods in its liturgical development, one in the sixteenth/seventeenth century, the other in the last 50 years. It is helpful at this point to describe briefly these two periods and the liturgical books that emerged from them, to which reference is made throughout this book.

From the sixteenth to the twentieth century

Most of the changes in the Church of England in the reign of Henry VIII were concerned more with church order than with worship. The authority of the King replaced that of the Pope. The monasteries were dissolved. Shrines were vandalized. But following these, Archbishop Thomas Cranmer (1489–1556) produced in 1549, in the reign of Edward VI, the First English Prayer Book. Looking back in the light of subsequent revisions, the 1549 Prayer Book appears a fairly conservative and catholic book but, at the time of its publication, it was experienced as a radical departure, not least because it was entirely in the English language. It was in use for only three years, when the Second English Prayer Book of 1552 took its place. This represented a huge theological shift and revealed the strong influence of the continental reformers with consequent liturgical changes, not least in the shape and language of the Eucharist. It was a thoroughgoing Protestant book.

But the people of England hardly had time to come to terms with it when the death of Edward VI in 1553 and the succession of his elder sister, Mary, the daughter of Henry's first queen, Catherine of Aragon, meant a return to Roman Catholicism and the Latin Mass. That, in its turn, was also short-lived, for Mary died in 1558 and was succeeded by her sister, Elizabeth, the daughter of Anne Boleyn. Elizabeth sought a middle way in terms of religion, but her Prayer Book differed little from that of 1552.

In the next century, the period of the Commonwealth after the execution of Charles I in 1649 saw the suppression of the Anglican liturgy, but with the restoration of the monarchy in 1660 came also the return of the English Prayer Book in 1662, in the definitive form in which it is still authorized and used: the Book of Common Prayer. After more than a hundred years of liturgical instability, the Church of England had a eucharistic liturgy that would last.

The Book of Common Prayer of 1662 became the staple diet of the Church of England for the next three centuries and the text of its service of Holy Communion invariable, at least in official provision. How it was celebrated and the frequency of celebration changed with each succeeding generation. Sometimes, at least in some places, there was a daily celebration, but in others a quarterly celebration. In some settings there was singing and elaborate ceremonial, in others plain and simple words and no music. Yet for all this variety, the words were a constant.

The twentieth century

The first serious attempt at reform was in the 1920s. A proposed Prayer Book that retained the 1662 Eucharist but also provided an alternative was brought before Parliament in 1927, rejected, brought back in 1928 and rejected again. Unofficially, and with the encouragement of the bishops, the 1928 proposal did nevertheless find wide usage for the following 40 years, though its Eucharistic Prayer, one of the reasons for its failure to pass through Parliament, was not frequently used. The Prayer Book as proposed in 1928 remains important in English liturgical history.

The passing of the Prayer Book (Alternative and Other Services) Measure of 1965 began the more recent round of liturgical revision in the Church of England. Influenced by the liturgical reforms in the Roman Catholic Church after the Second Vatican Council and by a broader worldwide liturgical movement, the Church of England recognized the need for liturgy that reflected both more recent scholarship and changing cultural conditions. In terms of the Eucharist, this meant a quick succession of new services. *An Order for Holy Communion (Alternative Services First Series)* came into force in 1967. Referred to as 'Series 1', in general it simply gave authority to deviations from 1662 that had been in use for some time, including much of what had featured in the 1928 rite. *An Order for Holy Communion (Alternative Services Second Series)*, a little blue pamphlet always known as 'Series 2', also authorized in 1967, returned the Eucharist to its pre-Reformation Western classic shape. Abandoning Thomas Cranmer's distinctive Reformation order, it simplified the texts but retained the Tudor English in which God was addressed as 'thee' and 'thou'. More radical was *An Order for Holy Communion (Alternative Services Series 3)*. Authorized six years later in 1973, it made the move into contemporary liturgical English. There were no major departures from the shape and structure of 'Series 2', but 'Series 3', because of the change of language, represented a significant shift in the worship of the Church of England.

The period of pamphlet liturgy was coming to an end. Work was already beginning on a complete, new service book and seven years later the Church of England had the end result: *The Alternative Service Book 1980 (ASB)*. Designated 'alternative' because it took its place alongside the Book of Common Prayer of 1662, rather than replacing it, it provided revisions of both 'Series 3', now called Rite A, and of 'Series 1' and 'Series 2', now brought together as a traditional language Rite B. Rite A was a more flexible rite than its predecessor, more complex too, and with increased seasonal provision in terms of Scripture sentences, prefaces and blessings. Authorized originally for ten years, it was re-authorized for a further ten, while work was going on to produce a rite for the new century.

In the year 2000 *Common Worship* replaced *ASB*. Holy Communion Order One is the natural successor to both Rite A and Rite B, existing in two forms, the first in contemporary liturgical language, the second retaining the language of 1662 and of Series 2. Holy Communion Order Two brings the 1662 rite, marginally revised, into *Common Worship* and also provides a contemporary language version of the Reformation order. Order One in contemporary language has become the normative eucharistic rite of the Church of England and there is no end-date fixed for its use, nor at present any plans for its revision. *Common Worship* may have extended considerably the range of services and celebrations authorized in the Church of England, but at its heart is a form of the Eucharist that has probably brought more unity of practice across the Church than has existed for a long time.

The story may seem complex, but it is important to hold on to the truth that the men and women who created these rites, and the prayers and other liturgical texts they contain, had only one object. It was, and is, to craft something beautiful that would draw people to the God who is revealed in Jesus Christ, that they might enter the mystery of God's being, find themselves caught up in the worship of heaven and have their lives shaped and transformed by Christ and the Christian gospel. And they simply could not achieve that without, in line after line, ensuring there were echoes of the words of Scripture.

There are two key words that will occur many times throughout this book in their Greek form, both because they are quite hard to put into English properly and because they are classic liturgical words. For those who have not come across them before they can sound confusing, but they are in fact relatively straightforward. These words are *epiclesis* and *anamnesis*. *Epiclesis* means 'calling down from on high' and refers to particular moments in the Eucharistic Prayers when the Spirit is called upon. *Anamnesis* means 'remembrance' and refers to the particular kind of remembrance that takes place in the Eucharist. For more on this word, see pages 31–2.

In what follows we have woven together the story of how the text came to be as it is with observations and reflections on how the Bible has been used and what is meant by the use of key words and phrases. There is much more that could have been said about the theology of the different parts of the Eucharist, but the aim of *Echoing the Word* is to be a small book that opens up thoughts and conversations about the theology of the eucharistic texts, not a book that says everything that could be said (if such a book could exist). We hope that the reflections and observations included in it will encourage people to be more attentive to the words they say week by week and, as a result, to reflect more deeply about what they believe as they come in worship before God.

1

Preparation and penitence

The liturgy begins with a greeting between the president and the people; in this greeting the community is gathered and bound together, and relationships are formed and acknowledged. The president may invoke the persons of the Trinity, proclaiming the worship to be offered to be in the name of Father, Son and Holy Spirit. There follows either the ancient and simplest of exchanges (bold text indicates a response from the whole congregation):

The Lord be with you
and also with you.

(which is discussed in Chapter 6 in relation to the Eucharistic Prayer) or else this more extended greeting:

Grace, mercy and peace
from God our Father
and the Lord Jesus Christ
be with you
and also with you.

The text is an extension of the greetings in 1 Timothy 1.2; 2 Timothy 1.2; and 2 John 1.3, and has roots far back in the early Church. The three words of the greeting sum up something about the essence of our relationship with God.

- 'Grace' is a hard word to tie down but it has a flavour of generosity and gift about it, and so hints at the many good things that we receive as a result of our life in Christ.
- 'Mercy', or 'compassion', refers to the nature of God always to reach out to us in love, no matter who we are or what we have done.

1

- 'Peace' not only evokes tranquillity but wholeness. The Hebrew word for 'peace', *shalom*, has a sense of completeness about it.

As we begin worship, then, the president and the congregation wish for each other an experience of God's generosity, compassion and wholeness that will underpin and inform everything else that is about to happen. Less formal words of welcome and introduction may follow, and in Eastertide the president adds the Easter acclamation ('Alleluia! Christ is risen').

The first prayer of the Eucharist is probably the oldest prayer composed in England still in use in the liturgy. The prayer of preparation, often called the 'Collect for Purity', is believed to be the work of Gregory, who was an abbot of Canterbury in the eighth century. Thomas Cranmer included it, to be said by the priest alone, in his First Prayer Book of 1549, and it has appeared in every English rite since, unaltered except for a change into contemporary language in 'Series 3'. From 'Series 2' onwards it has been optional and, when said, is now nearly always said by the congregation, rather than by the priest alone.

The two emphases of the prayer – on preparation and purity – combine in its major focus, which is that of calling down the Holy Spirit upon the celebration. In the earlier liturgies, where there was no explicit *epiclesis* (or invocation of the Spirit, see pages xv and 29) in the Eucharistic Prayer, this prayer could be considered an *epiclesis* for the whole rite, so that the Holy Spirit could be seen as enabling both the prayers that were offered and the presence of Christ to be experienced.

The prayer picks up the plea of the psalmist in Psalm 51 that God will cleanse his sins (vv. 2, 7), give him a clean heart (v. 10) and refrain from taking his Holy Spirit away (v. 11). This becomes conflated in this prayer into a cleansing of the thoughts of our hearts by the Holy Spirit. What is intriguing is that the author of the prayer has introduced into it the Hebraic notion that we think with our hearts, rather than with our brains or

2

our minds. As a result, the prayer then becomes much closer to the Sermon on the Mount (see especially Matthew 5.27–30), in which Jesus reminds us that what we think about can be as sinful as the actual things that we do.

> **Almighty God,**
> **to whom all hearts are open,**
> **all desires known,**
> **and from whom no secrets are hidden:**
> **cleanse the thoughts of our hearts**
> **by the inspiration of your Holy Spirit,**
> **that we may perfectly love you,**
> **and worthily magnify your holy name;**
> **through Christ our Lord.**

Following this prayer, the service moves from preparation to penitence. A general confession by the whole congregation came quite late into the eucharistic liturgy, but it has been a part of the Anglican tradition since 1549. There this general confession was to be made 'in the name of all those that are minded to receive the Holy Communion, either by one of them, or else by one of the ministers, or by the priest himself, all humbly kneeling upon their knees.' In that First Prayer Book, as in subsequent liturgies until 1980, it was placed as a response to the reading and preaching of the word (in 1549 after the prayer of consecration, but from 1552 before it), but a note of penitence was struck at the beginning of the service by the reading of the Ten Commandments. *The Alternative Service Book 1980 (ASB)* allowed for the prayers of penitence to come either as part of the Gathering, the introductory part of the Eucharist from the Greeting to the Collect, or in the established place after the prayers of intercession. But a rite in which they were printed twice was confusing and *Common Worship* has opted for the earlier point, so that they become essentially part of the preparation for worship. There is much optional material, allowing this part of the liturgy to be quite brief or quite extended.

In its most extensive form it makes use of much biblical material to set the scene and introduce the confession. The Commandments (Exodus 20.1–17) may be used as they stand or in a modified form that places alongside each commandment a New Testament text that may be seen as commentary or even a Christian corrective. The Beatitudes (Matthew 5.1–10) appear as an alternative for the first time in *Common Worship*. The so-called 'Comfortable Words', which Cranmer had taken from the continental reformers Archbishop Hermann von Wied of Cologne and Ulrich Zwingli in Zurich, are direct words of Scripture: Matthew 11.28; John 3.16; 1 Timothy 1.15; and 1 John 2.1–2.

But the most frequent biblical preface to confession lies in what has come to be called the 'Summary of the Law'. This is the one text printed in the main service, while the others are indicated by a rubric but printed outside the main service. The Summary of the Law merges Matthew's (22.37–40) and Mark's (12.29–31) versions. One of the key differences between the two versions in Matthew and Mark is what we love the Lord with – in Matthew it is heart, soul and mind; in Mark it is heart, soul, mind and strength. The original version in Deuteronomy 6.5 had heart, soul and might. The reason for the change may well be connected to the issue raised by the prayer of preparation. In Hebraic thinking the heart was the seat of rational thought, so the original Deuteronomy passage referred to loving God with rational thought, with what makes us alive (i.e. our soul) and with great effort (i.e. our might). When this was translated into Greek thought the notion of worshipping God with our reason was lost – since in Greek thought the heart is the seat of emotion, not of thinking; so mind was added to ensure that reason was maintained. In some versions it replaced might, but in others both stayed. The intriguing implication of this is that a new means of worshipping God was introduced into the Summary of the Law: worshipping with our emotions too.

Although there is considerable variety possible, none of these biblical texts is required to be read. At its most simple a minister, using one of a variety of possible brief texts or something more spontaneous, invites the people to confess their sins. They respond with a prayer of confession. The president says a prayer of absolution.

Among the invitations to confession, the 'default' form, first written for the 'Series 3' rite, draws on ideas and phrases present in the Comfortable Words:

> God so loved the world
> that he gave his only Son Jesus Christ
> to save us from our sins,
> to be our advocate in heaven,
> and to bring us to eternal life.
>
> Let us confess our sins in penitence and faith,
> firmly resolved to keep God's commandments
> and to live in love and peace with all.

This introduction stitches together a variety of passages that, when combined, seem to sum up who Jesus was and what he came to do. The base verse is, of course, John 3.16, which tops and tails the sentiment of the invitation; the reason why we are here at all is because of God's overwhelming love, which led him to give his Son so that those who believe in him might have eternal life. The context of this well-known verse is important. Around this verse, Jesus mentions Moses' lifting up of the snake in the desert and compares it to his own lifting up on the cross. Implicit in the conversation is the assertion that we have to lift our eyes beyond our own earthly conditions (John 3.12) in order to be able to see, comprehend and believe in Jesus who has been sent down from heaven.

Given that, this is the perfect verse to use at this point in the service. One of the ways in which sin holds us captive is that we become so absorbed in it and in our inability to act otherwise that we forget to raise our eyes to the one who loves us so deeply. These words of invitation, then, remind us of the importance of lifting our eyes to God before we confess our sins.

Added into John 3.16 here are resonances of a number of other verses that broaden and deepen the theology about Christ that is given at this point. The first and third elements ('save us from our sins' and 'bring us to eternal life') are arguably implicit in John 3.16 already, but the second is an intriguing departure. The phrase, 'to be our advocate in heaven', weaves together 1 John 2.1 ('if anyone does sin, we have an advocate with the Father, Jesus Christ the righteous') with Job 16.19 ('Even now, in fact, my witness is in heaven, and he that vouches for me is on high'), explicitly locating the advocate in heaven, reminding us that the one who chose human form has now taken our humanity to the heart of the Godhead and there pleads on our behalf. The introduction of these three elements draws our attention to the past, present and future. Jesus *was* the one who came to save his people from their sins, he *is* the one who acts as our advocate in heaven and he *will be* the one who brings us to eternal life.

These simple, yet beautiful, words give us the context in which we come to confession with our eyes lifted to Christ who has been, is and will be the one who saves us from our sins.

There are a number of forms of the confession prayer, most of them in the supplementary material, and we must be content to explore the two in the main text. The first is this:

> **Almighty God, our heavenly Father,**
> **we have sinned against you**
> **and against our neighbour**
> **in thought and word and deed,**
> **through negligence, through weakness,**
> **through our own deliberate fault.**
> **We are truly sorry**
> **and repent of all our sins.**
> **For the sake of your Son Jesus Christ,**

who died for us,
forgive us all that is past
and grant that we may serve you in newness of life
to the glory of your name.

The prayer has gone through a number of changes in its comparatively short history. Newly composed for 'Series 2' in 1967, it drew in its first part on the traditional preparation prayers of the Roman Mass and in the second part was a simplification of the confession in the Book of Common Prayer. But the 1967 version was thought to be too short and lacking in sorrow for sin. Subsequent revisions in 'Series 3' and *ASB* added material to meet that criticism, and *Common Worship* made only one simple change from 'fellow men' to 'neighbour' in the interests of gender inclusivity. It remains a well-crafted, straightforward text, the most commonly used of the confessions, but not perhaps the most poetic and certainly light on Scripture.

Indeed one of the intriguing features of this confession is that, although it might sound biblical, the resonances with Scripture are at best allusive and indirect. The opening phrases probably have the richest scriptural resonance, drawing on the language of the Old Testament where God is described as mighty (which occurs so often it is not worth giving a reference for) along with New Testament language referring to God as our heavenly Father. (Although God is described in the Old Testament as being like a Father to Israel, there is no doubt that in the New Testament Jesus takes this one step further and invites us to join him in addressing God as 'Father'.)

Following this, the prayer echoes the confession of the prodigal son in Luke 15.21 to his father that he has sinned against him, though it omits the reference to heaven and instead speaks of sinning against our neighbours. This is something that can be traced to Leviticus 19.18, which, as well as the more familiar command to love our neighbours as ourselves, also forbids taking vengeance or holding a grudge against our neighbours. The final phrase, 'newness of life', may well be drawn from

Romans 6.4, though the context is different. Romans 6.4 talks of dying and rising with Christ in baptism to newness of life, whereas the confession does not make this overt link.

The rest of the confession contains little that is overtly biblical, though of course the recognition that God's forgiveness of our sins is because of Jesus' death is a central concept in Paul's writings.

Not so the alternative that follows it in *Common Worship*:

Most merciful God,
Father of our Lord Jesus Christ,
we confess that we have sinned
in thought, word and deed.
We have not loved you with our whole heart.
We have not loved our neighbours as ourselves.
In your mercy
forgive what we have been,
help us to amend what we are,
and direct what we shall be;
that we may do justly,
love mercy,
and walk humbly with you, our God.

The reason for the inclusion of a second prayer is itself interesting. Submissions from members of the General Synod argued, in relation to the first prayer, that we cannot sin against our neighbours, only against God. Without arguing the point, the Liturgical Commission, looking for an alternative text, turned to a prayer that had formed the confession in *Morning and Evening Prayer Alternative Services Second Series (Revised)* and which, before that, had featured in Presbyterian and ecumenical orders but had disappeared in subsequent Anglican provision. It draws on Micah 6.8. The Commission added the line 'Father of our Lord Jesus Christ', with echoes of the 1662 confession, and recast the final line to give a stronger ending: 'with you, our God' instead of 'with thee'. Failure to love our neighbours has replaced sin against our neighbours.

As a result, this text is the more profoundly biblical and theological. As with the other confession, the prayer opens with an address to God that combines both Old and New Testament themes.

It is interesting to note that probably the two most common epithets for God in the Old Testament are 'almighty' and 'merciful'. Some might argue that they sum up two of the key elements of God's nature: his might and his compassion. It is therefore even more intriguing to notice that one confession opts for one of these epithets and the other for the other; though 'merciful' is, arguably, more appropriate than 'almighty' in the context of a confession. Alongside this Old Testament allusion is 'Father of our Lord Jesus Christ', a common New Testament description of God who is Christ's Father and, as a result, also ours.

This is then followed by a confession of our failure to keep the law in even its summary form (that we should love God and our neighbours) and a plea that God should transform us so that, for the future, we can live up to that which God requires of us as set out in Micah 6.8. One of the key features of this prayer, in fact, is that it focuses as much on the future as on the past with the wish that we might amend our lives to do better in the future than we have done to this point.

We need to look now at the *Kyrie eleison*, a little Greek text, with its English translation, 'Lord, have mercy', that found its way back into the Anglican Eucharist in 1928 and has been an option in every rite since. It is all that is left of a longer litany of intercession going back to the fourth century. The meaning did not originally have a specific penitential tone. Intercessory in character, it had more of a sense of 'Lord, look with kindness', similar in meaning to 'Hear our prayer'. Indeed the Hebrew word for 'mercy' is connected to the word for 'womb' and has the resonance of tender care and nurture, meaning that we are asking God to look with compassion upon us.

It was Cranmer's rendering of it in 1549 as 'Lord, have mercy *upon us*' (emphasis added) that began to give it a more penitential flavour. Its use in 'Series 3', where it is an alternative to the *Gloria in excelsis*, strengthened that emphasis. *Common Worship* has taken it a stage further, following the contemporary Roman Mass by allowing its use with the interpolation of penitential sentences of Scripture to turn it into a confession. But in the end, the cry, *Kyrie, eleison, Christe, eleison* is something broader and deeper than simply a desire to be forgiven our sins.

The prayers of penitence reach their natural conclusion in a prayer of absolution. Although there are other authorized texts, only one is included in the main service order. It is still recognizable as the text that Cranmer devised in 1549, although small changes have been made, most significantly in 1967, when 'bring you to everlasting life' became 'keep you in life eternal'.

> Almighty God,
> who forgives all who truly repent,
> have mercy upon *you*,
> pardon and deliver *you* from all *your* sins,
> confirm and strengthen *you* in all goodness,
> and keep *you* in life eternal;
> through Jesus Christ our Lord.

The shift from the phrase 'bring you to everlasting life' to 'keep you in life eternal' to some extent represents changing theological fashions and an emphasis in the late twentieth century on eternal life as having begun in the here and now, rather than as something to come beyond death. The differences between the two versions appear to be marked, although in a sense each captures a different important element.

Before we can address the whole phrase, it is worth reflecting briefly on the word that is variously translated as 'everlasting' or 'eternal'. This hugely important word – it occurs over 70 times in the New Testament – is notoriously difficult to translate. It means literally 'related to the age' or 'lasting the age long'. The contexts in which it is used make it clear that it refers not to this age, which will come to an end, but to the future age that will never end. Thus life that lasts the age long is 'everlasting' or 'eternal'. But one could argue that this is not its most important characteristic. The life that both Jesus and Paul are talking about is life fit for the age to come, an age ruled perfectly by God, undergirded by justice, peace and compassion. In other words it is the quality, not the length, of the life that is key. As a result, 'eternal' may be a marginally better translation than 'everlasting', but neither term quite encompasses the original meaning.

The second issue is whether we are 'brought to' or 'kept in' this life. Again, to a certain extent both are true. We do not yet inhabit the life of the age to come in all its fullness, and we will be brought to it at our life's end. Nevertheless, as both the Gospels and Paul's letters make clear, on a number of occasions this life has already broken in. It is part of the mystery of life in Christ that the life of the age to come is both ours and beyond our grasp all at the same time. For this reason, 'keep you in life eternal' may be slightly preferable to 'bring you to everlasting life', but neither phrase can quite communicate the enormity of the theology that it is trying to convey.

The absolution spoken, penitence can be left behind and, at least on Sundays and festival days, the community can now break into a joyful song of praise.

2

Gloria in excelsis

Glory to God in the highest,
and peace to his people on earth.

Lord God, heavenly King,
almighty God and Father,
we worship you, we give you thanks,
we praise you for your glory.

Lord Jesus Christ, only Son of the Father,
Lord God, Lamb of God,
you take away the sin of the world:
have mercy on us;
you are seated at the right hand of the Father:
receive our prayer.

For you alone are the Holy One,
you alone are the Lord,
you alone are the Most High, Jesus Christ,
with the Holy Spirit,
in the glory of God the Father.
Amen.

The *Gloria in excelsis* began its life not in the Eucharist but in
Morning Prayer. Its authorship is unknown but it appears to
go back to the fourth century. It was used in both East and West
in the morning and it retains that position as part of Morning
Prayer in the Eastern churches. But around the beginning
of the sixth century, Pope Symmachus (498–514) brought it
into the text of the Eucharist, though initially only on Sundays
and the feasts of martyrs, and then only when the bishop was
presiding. Thus it established itself in the Roman order of the
Mass, though its use was restricted. Until the twelfth century

its use by priests was restricted to Easter. From that point onwards it gradually found its way into the eucharistic order every Sunday, except in penitential seasons and on a variety of feast days. Its position was always near the beginning of the liturgy, a burst of praise before settling into prayer (summed up in the Collect) and the reading of the Scriptures.

In the Church of England, and therefore in an English translation by Thomas Cranmer, it appears for the first time in 1549. It is a slightly condensed version of the established text, with the loss of some of the repetitions. 'Lamb of God', 'have mercy upon us' and 'receive our prayer' all feature only once in the text. It is to be said or sung by 'the clerkes' at the traditional point at the beginning of the Eucharist.

Three years later, in 1552, it has moved to a quite novel place in the service, right at the end, just before the blessing. Its move was part of Cranmer's radical shaping of the order of the Eucharist to reflect the theology he had adopted. Only when the community had shared in the bread and wine of Holy Communion did the service, until then restrained and strong on human unworthiness, take off into thanksgiving and praise. The *Gloria* as the climax of that was natural enough. The Book of Common Prayer of 1662 leaves it in that position and orders its use at every celebration, making no distinction about penitential seasons.

In the liturgical renewal of the last 50 years, a number of things have changed. First of all, there was an attempt to bring the *Gloria* back into Morning Prayer. First advocated by the Liturgical Commission in 1966, it found its way into Morning Prayer as an alternative to the *Te Deum*. This was quite logical, for it comes from the same genre of praise canticle. In some of the revisions it was allocated a day of its own – Thursday – irrespective of season. By the time of *ASB* that particular innovation had established itself, at least in the Shorter Form of Morning Prayer, by now using the international and ecumenical ICET (International Consultation on English Texts) text. But its use through the centuries as a text for the Eucharist and its frequent use with that service meant that people were reluctant to take it back into Morning Prayer. Whatever the historical precedents, it seemed to have established itself as belonging to the Eucharist, which, after 1,400 years, seems very reasonable! So the Church of England's *Common Worship Daily Prayer* does not include it in Morning Prayer, except as a possible additional canticle at the end of the office on special feasts.

It is in the Eucharist that it belongs, but where and how often? In 1967, for the first time since Cranmer had moved it to the end of the Eucharist, Anglicans were permitted to restore it to its place at the beginning of the service. 'Series 2', while continuing to use many of Cranmer's texts, abandoned his radical reshaping of the Eucharist and returned to the classic ecumenical shape. As part of that, 1662's long climax of thanksgiving after Communion gave way to a short, sharp ending of the rite in sending out for mission. The *Gloria* did not fit there and returned to its older place. In 1971, with 'Series 3', it acquired a new translation, and in subsequent revisions in 1980 and 2000 it has stayed in that same place, always at the beginning, but always optional.

'Series 3' had made it an alternative to *Kyrie eleison* ('Lord, have mercy') and, though this was not clearly stated, the implication was that *Kyrie eleison* was a penitential text and the *Gloria* a festal alternative. Although they are no longer set out as alternatives, that is the way they are often understood and, as far as Sunday liturgy is concerned, the contemporary norm is the singing of the *Gloria*, except in Advent and Lent, when *Kyrie eleison* takes its place. *Common Worship* in its main text says that 'The *Gloria in excelsis* may be used', though a note spells the matter out more clearly: 'This canticle may be omitted during Advent and Lent, and on weekdays which are not Principal Holy Days or Festivals.'

So here it is, an ancient song, finding a place in the Eucharist through most of its history, enabling Christian people in their liturgy to mark the beginning of their gathering with a burst of praise. The fact that it is a song is important. As a spoken text it cannot be as effective as when sung. Whether sung or said, it begins with the song of the angels and then breaks into three acclamations, the first to the Father, and the second and third to the Son, but drawn together in a doxology that celebrates also the Holy Spirit, so that it ends in the celebration of the Trinity.

It is also a song steeped in Scripture; indeed so deep and wide are its resonances with Scripture that it is only possible to give a sample of the potential references that could be seen to stand behind the text. One of the interesting features of the song is that, although it is clearly Trinitarian, it is only just so. The two long expressions of praise to God the Father and God the Son are hardly balanced with the very brief 'with the Holy Spirit'.

The first paragraph sets the tone for the whole song with the song of the angels to the shepherds in Luke's Gospel. This phrase establishes something of vast theological importance that forms the backdrop to not only our praise in this song but the whole of our lives as Christians. The prophecies of Isaiah looked forward to a time when the nations of the earth would see God's glory (e.g. Isaiah 40.5) and would live in peace (e.g. Isaiah 11.1–10). The message of the angels to the shepherds was that this time had come: God's glory could now be seen and humanity could live in peace and wholeness. We begin our praise, therefore, with a reminder of this.

This naturally flows into praise of that God whose glory we can now behold. The song uses four titles for God. The only one worthy of especial comment is 'heavenly King' which, though implicit throughout much of the Old Testament (in that God sits on a throne in heaven), is only stated explicitly once, in Daniel 4.37, where God is called 'King of heaven'.

The second paragraph turns our attention to Jesus Christ and uses titles for him, particularly from John's Gospel. It is worth noticing that the *Gloria* here makes explicit the connection between having mercy on us and receiving our prayer because we ask Jesus to do both. We ask for mercy on the basis of his earthly ministry – to be the one who takes away the sins of the world (John 1.29) – and now because of his place in heaven to receive our prayer. The reference to Jesus Christ sitting at the right hand of the Father is vastly important but is, nevertheless, a piece of New Testament shorthand that it is easy to overlook. In that short phrase is embedded some hugely important theology. The longhand version of this phrase would read something like: 'God raised him from the dead and exalted him to heaven at the Ascension, where he now dwells with God on his throne, taking our human nature into the heart of the Godhead and acting there as our permanent advocate with the Father.' It is such an important phrase that it is dotted throughout the New Testament. In this particular context you need to see the longhand version to comprehend the significance of requesting that Jesus receive our prayer. It is because he sits at the right hand of the Father that he can.

The *Gloria*, then, reminds us of Jesus' humanity and divinity, earthly sojourn and heavenly location. He has carried our humanity into the very heart of the Godhead and as a result both listens to us with compassion and love and intercedes on our behalf.

3

The Peace

Between the *Gloria* and 'the Peace' falls the ministry of the word, which we will not be exploring here. As a result, the next part of the eucharistic service for exploration is the Peace.

The greeting of peace reflects Scripture in two ways, partly because the warrant for it is very clear in the New Testament and partly because in the liturgy it is usually introduced by direct quotation from the Bible.

Its origins lie in the letters of Paul and Peter. In Romans 16.16 Paul writes, 'Greet one another with a holy kiss. All the churches of Christ greet you.' He writes something similar in 1 Corinthians 16.20; 2 Corinthians 13.12; and 1 Thessalonians 5.26. In 1 Peter 5.14 the writer invites the readers to greet one another 'with a kiss of love'. Whether such a greeting was, at that stage, a formal liturgical action, we cannot know, but by the time of Justin Martyr in the second century it has clearly moved into a liturgical setting. 'At the conclusion of the prayers we greet one another with a kiss', he writes in his *First Apology* around the year 155. The prayers to which he refers are, as in contemporary orders, after the reading of the Scriptures and before the preparation of the gifts. Origen and Tertullian, both writing only a little later, also speak of the Peace as part of the liturgy. Tertullian understands it as 'the seal of prayer'.

Justin, Origen and Tertullian all point not only to the inclusion of the greeting of peace in the Eucharist but to this position between the prayers and the offertory. As to why it is found in exactly that place, the answer probably lies in the words of Jesus in Matthew 5.23–24:

So when you are offering your gift at the altar, if you remember
that your brother or sister has something against you, leave your
gift there before the altar and go; first be reconciled to your
brother or sister, and then come and offer your gift.

But there is another position for the Peace, which goes back
to at least the fifth century in Rome, where it comes after the
Eucharistic Prayer as part of the immediate preparation for
Communion. Here it is more associated with the prayer for
forgiveness in the Lord's Prayer and with the prayer for peace
in the anthem 'Lamb of God'. This is the place in the liturgy
that it has retained in the Roman Mass.

The Peace is both a text and a gesture. The text is invariable.
'The peace of the Lord be always with you' invites the response
'and with your spirit', loosely rendered more often 'and also
with you'. The phrase itself is not biblical but, as well as the
many references given above, it probably most resonates with
Jesus' resurrection greeting to the disciples in John 20, where
he says, literally, 'Peace with you' three times (vv. 19, 21, 26).
The lack of a verb makes it unclear whether he meant 'Peace
is already with you' or 'May peace be with you.' As is often the
case, it may well be that both meanings are caught up in the
phrase. As a result of who Jesus was and what Jesus did, peace
is already ours, but Jesus' wish is that we live it out, experience
it and be conscious of it.

'Peace' is such an important word it is probably worth repeating that, as well as the more popular modern senses of the
word – that of calmness or tranquillity – the biblical use of
'peace' suggests wholeness and completeness (this is certainly
what the Hebrew word *shalom* means). When he greeted his
disciples, then, Jesus was not declaring or wishing tranquillity
for them but a completion of their being, a wholeness that
meant they could understand what peace really meant.

The gesture accompanying the words of the Peace has varied
from century to century and culture to culture. The holy kiss
can sometimes be the holy hug or the holy handshake!

In terms of its Anglican history, the words, without any gesture, are in 1549, but have disappeared in 1552, returning as an option in 1928, in both cases in the 'Roman' position before the distribution. 'Series 2' makes it mandatory and moves it to the classic position before the offertory, where it is also following on from the prayers of penitence and the prayer of humble access, but still has no mention of gesture. 'Series 3' goes a little further, for it says that the president 'gives' the Peace as he says the words. From *ASB* onwards a minister may add, 'Let us offer one another a sign of peace' and 'All may exchange a sign of peace.' In *Common Worship*, where the prayers of penitence have moved to the beginning of the rite and the prayer of humble access to a place immediately before the distribution, the Peace now stands, as it did for Tertullian, as the seal of the prayers and the preface to the preparation of the gifts.

In most rites the simple exchange between president and people suffices, but in the English rites since 'Series 2' there have been Bible sentences to introduce the Peace. Interestingly these have not included the verse from Matthew 5 or the Pauline sentences that provide a warrant for 'the kiss of peace', but sentences that more generally encourage the unity of Christians.

'Series 2' has 'We are the body of Christ. By one Spirit we were all baptized into one Body. Endeavour to keep the unity of the Spirit in the bond of peace.' The first sentence draws on 1 Corinthians 12, refashioning verses 13 and 27. The second sentence moves to Ephesians and makes use of Ephesians 4.3.

'Series 3' replaced the second sentence with 'Let us then pursue all that makes for peace and builds up our common life' from Romans 14.19. *ASB* provided an alternative text, a pastiche drawing on Ephesians 2.14, 16; Matthew 18.20; and 1 Thessalonians 5.13: 'Christ is our peace. He has reconciled us to God in one body by the cross. We meet in his name and share his peace.'

Common Worship, desiring that no particular text should establish itself to the exclusion of others, provides no sentence in the main order but gives both the *ASB* sentences, together with many others, some of them seasonal, in the Supplementary Texts. The reason for these extra sentences is that they all point back to the extra meaning of 'peace' that we referred to above. They all, in their own way, seek to explain something about the peace we are talking about here. It is a peace, a wholeness, that arises out of our common life together in Christ, a life that Christ established by his death and resurrection and, as a result, is no abstract idea. This peace must be lived out in the lives of all those who call themselves Christians.

In the greeting of peace, especially with the extended texts and with an 'exchange' of greeting, the congregation is engaged in one of two activities. Sometimes it is giving expression to a deep sense of belonging one to another that is already well established. But in another setting it may be using the Peace to deepen a sense of community that may not be too firmly established. Sometimes the Peace reflects community; sometimes it forms it. Always it is celebrating something about reconciliation. It is – to use Tertullian's word – 'sealing' its prayers in a symbolic action and in a new greeting that is richer than the initial 'The Lord be with you'. Although its use has extended to non-eucharistic settings, it is within the Eucharist and at this moment that the Peace speaks most tellingly, moving the assembly into a new and deeper experience of fellowship as it takes bread and wine and makes ready to meet the Lord in his sacramental presence.

4

Prayers at the preparation of the table

Are there suitable words that help prepare the worshipper for the great Eucharistic Prayer? The pre-Reformation Church thought so and provided prayers that spoke of offering. The Reformation swept these away and instead gave Bible sentences that focused on the giving of money, rather than the offering of bread and wine. There have been two objections to the pre-Reformation prayers. The first is that their use of the language of offering in the Eucharist detracts from the unique self-offering of Jesus on the cross (and this is discussed on pages 71–5). The second is that almost any words one might choose to use about the bread and wine at this moment might seem to anticipate and therefore to undermine the Eucharistic Prayer itself.

So Thomas Cranmer in 1549 provided instead 20 biblical texts, focusing on money and generous giving, including two from the Apocrypha (Tobit 4), and 1552 and 1662 left these unchanged. None of these is a prayer, and none of them applies to bread and wine. The first and most commonly used has been 'Let your light so shine before men, that they may see your good works, and glorify your Father which is in heaven' (Matthew 5.16 KJV).

The proposed Prayer Book of 1928 very gently reintroduced the possibility that the offertory is concerned with bread and wine and not just with money by adding two further sentences: 'I will offer in his dwelling an oblation with great gladness: I will sing and speak praises unto the Lord' (Psalm 27.6, Coverdale) and 'Melchizedek king of Salem brought forth bread and wine: and he was the priest of the most high God' (Genesis 14.18 KJV).

'Series 1' marked the first introduction of a text from 1 Chronicles 29.11–14 which, though a straight quotation from Scripture, is a prayer, offered by King David. In 'Series 1' it followed the placing of bread and wine upon the holy table. It disappeared, as did any text at this point, in 'Series 2'. In 'Series 3' it returned in relation to the presentation of bread and wine. In *ASB* it was associated with 'the offerings of the people', but it was unclear whether these offerings included bread and wine or simply described the offerings 'collected'. In *Common Worship* the text remains, though the wording is in more contemporary English:

> Yours, Lord, is the greatness, the power,
> the glory, the splendour and the majesty;
> for everything in heaven and on earth is yours.
> **All things come from you,**
> **and of your own do we give you.**

Because it was the only text provided through the years of 'Series 3' and *ASB*, it has achieved the status of a norm, despite now being relegated to the supplementary material where it is only one of a variety of forms. It is a clever text to draw into the Eucharist, for it engages helpfully with the tension between the fact that we do bring our gifts to God – whether the bread and wine or the money that, in different ways, stand for human labour and daily life – and the fact that, to paraphrase a line from the old hymn 'Rock of Ages', 'nothing in our hands we bring'; we come simply holding out empty hands to receive from a gracious God. At a certain level we have nothing to offer.

The 1 Chronicles text (1 Chronicles 29.11) comes from the passage that describes King David's preparation for the building of the Temple. Although David was prevented from building the Temple, 1 Chronicles recounts his desire to provide goods to enable Solomon to do what he himself could not do. The prayer accompanies his offering of these gifts and in it he makes clear that he is fully aware that what he offers is itself a gift from God. As a result, this prayer is well placed, here, in the service and affirms that we bring something, but what we bring is itself a gift from God.

Something of the theological tension around the whole question of offering is to be found in the Anglican approach to the offertory prayers of the Roman Mass. With resonances of Jewish table prayers and with a compelling flow and beauty, Anglicans have been attracted to them through several decades.

The opening of these prayers, 'Blessed are you, Lord God . . .' is a characteristically Jewish form of prayer, and the wording of these blessings resonates strongly with some of the Jewish Shabbat prayers, such as:

- 'Blessed are you, Lord our God, King of the Universe, who brings forth bread from the earth.'
- 'Blessed are you, Lord our God, King of the Universe, who creates the fruit of the vine.'

This has the very helpful effect of reminding us that the Eucharist, though now very different in form, has at least some roots in the Shabbat service.

However, the form of these prayers in the Eucharist, beginning as they do with reference to 'offering', has, for some at least, seemed theologically mistaken, at least at this particular point in the service. *ASB* dealt with the issue by a subtle rubric that stated that 'the president may praise God for his gifts in appropriate words to which all respond **Blessed be God for ever**', leaving the priest to recognize this as a green light to use the Roman texts although they were not printed. *Common Worship*, however, as with the 1 Chronicles prayer, prints them, with other prayers at the preparation of the table, in the Supplementary Texts, but with a significant change.

Blessed are you, Lord God of all creation:
through your goodness we have this bread to set before you,
which earth has given and human hands have made.
It will become for us the bread of life.
Blessed be God for ever.

Blessed are you, Lord God of all creation:
through your goodness we have this wine to set before you,
fruit of the vine and work of human hands.
It will become for us the cup of salvation.
Blessed be God for ever.

The significant change is from the language of offering to that of bread and wine that we 'set before' God.

One other of the prayers has a significant prehistory. It is based on a text in the *Didache*, the date of which is unknown, though it is probably from the late first century and perhaps from Syria. The prayer has a strong emphasis on the expectation of the end times and reflects the anticipation of the consummation of all things in Christ that so inspired the first Christians.

As the grain once scattered in the fields
and the grapes once dispersed on the hillside
are now reunited on this table in bread and wine,
so, Lord, may your whole Church soon be gathered together
from the corners of the earth
into your kingdom.

The other nine prayers are of modern composition. Two focus specifically on money, others on the bread and wine, while others look forward more openly to what is to follow. Most of these were newly written by Michael Vasey for the *Common Worship* rite. His intention, and that of the Commission, was to avoid the pitfall of prayers that seemed to anticipate the later 'oblation' of Christ (see pages 75–6) and to create quite gentle, low-key prayers in contrast to the great Eucharistic Prayer that would follow; texts that would, so to speak, prepare the way. Among them are these:

> Be present, be present,
> Lord Jesus Christ,
> our risen high priest;
> make yourself known in the breaking of bread.

This prayer combines the vision of the book of Hebrews that sees the risen Jesus as now being the High Priest in the heavenly Temple (Hebrews 4.14), with the well-loved story of the road to Emmaus, where Jesus was made known to the two disciples in the breaking of the bread (Luke 24.35). It draws together the themes of Jesus transcendent and immanent; glorious in heaven and walking alongside us in our incomprehension.

> Wise and gracious God,
> you spread a table before us;
> nourish your people with the word of life
> and the bread of heaven.

Here we find a combination of the theme of the messianic banquet with the Johannine language of Jesus as the bread of heaven (John 6.58). The messianic banquet is a theme that runs beneath the surface throughout much of the Old and New Testaments. The vision is one in which God invites us to share with him in a rich feast with the Messiah in the blessed age of the world to come. A theme that runs through much of eucharistic liturgy is the belief that every time we celebrate the last supper as Jesus commanded us to do, we have a foretaste of that rich and satisfying banquet.

> Blessed be God,
> who feeds the hungry,
> who raises the poor,
> who fills our praise.

In this prayer we find a simple summary of the nature of God. Its opening, with the characteristically Jewish phrase 'Blessed be God', gives the prayer a Hebraic tone that is fulfilled in the three short phrases that could each be drawn from a number of Old Testament sources; see for example Psalm 107.9; 1 Samuel 2.8; Psalm 48.10. Although many more phrases could be used to describe God's nature, these three provide an excellent start for our reflections about God. The description of God's nature is also Hebraic in that it does not use abstract nouns to describe who God is but points to his actions: what God does tells us who he is.

Although all these prayers are direct and simple, each contains a profound theology that attempts to encapsulate something of the wonder of what we are about to do.

5

The shape of the Eucharistic Prayer

Clearly the most significant texts within the Eucharist are the
Eucharistic Prayers themselves. Until 1980 each eucharistic
rite had only one Eucharistic Prayer; there was no element of
choice. But from 1980 there was choice. In Rite A of *ASB*
there were four prayers. In the main text of *Common Worship*
Order One there are eight. This has introduced considerable
textual variety. But except in two matters, one more significant
than the other, there has been no equivalent variety of shape.
So it is helpful at this early point in our book to indicate that
shape and then, to a great extent, to take it for granted in the
ten chapters that look at the texts of the prayers. It may also
be helpful to introduce at this point just a few fairly technical
liturgical words relating to Eucharistic Prayers and then to be
able to use them without explanation at later points in the
book.

The classic shape of a Eucharistic Prayer as found in most
contemporary liturgies in the West is this:

Opening dialogue
Preface
'Holy, holy, holy . . . Blessed is he . . .'
Praying for the Spirit upon the gifts
Institution narrative
Memorial acclamation
Calling to mind the mighty acts
Prayer for fruitful reception / Prayer for the Spirit upon the people
Intercession
Doxology
Amen

In the following paragraphs we address each of these in turn, in some cases very briefly, simply referring the reader to material later in the book.

The opening dialogue is a six-line exchange between president and people with which the prayer begins. Its text is identical in all the prayers. It is often called by the Latin name *Sursum Corda*, which is the Latin equivalent of its third line, 'Lift up your hearts'. It is discussed below in Chapter 6.

The preface takes the prayer from its opening exchange through to the next congregational text: 'Holy, holy, holy, Lord'. It is always a prayer of thanksgiving, picking up and expanding the last two lines of the dialogue.

> Let us give thanks to the Lord our God.
> **It is right to give thanks and praise.**

This can take one of two forms. The 'thanksgiving', as its name suggests, gives thanks to God for what he has done in Creation, in the sending of Jesus, in the death and resurrection of Jesus, in the sending of the Holy Spirit and in the creation of the Church. This is often called the 'common preface'. Alternatively, instead of or in addition to this common preface there may be, for any feast or season, a 'proper' preface that focuses instead on what that feast or season celebrates rather than on the whole story of redemption. In the Book of Common Prayer, the common preface is minimal, but on five principal feast days – and in some cases on the seven days after as well – there is a proper preface that teaches something about the particular mystery the Church is celebrating on that day.

Subsequent liturgies have done two things. They have made the common preface longer, ensuring that those activities of God in Creation, in Jesus, in the Spirit and in the Church are named and celebrated, and they have increased considerably the number of days for which a proper preface can or should be added. *Common Worship* has gone one stage further by dividing prefaces into two categories: 'short prefaces' that are added to a common preface and 'extended prefaces' that replace the common preface and focus entirely on the feast or season. Some of these are original compositions, some adapt earlier versions, and some are drawn from the new Roman Catholic Sacramentary.

What all prefaces have in common is at least one final clause catching up the praises of the community into the praises of the angels and saints, sometimes linked with the praises of all Creation, in words such as:

> with angels and archangels,
> and with all the company of heaven,
> we proclaim your great and glorious name,
> for ever praising you and *saying*...
> (Common Preface, Prayers A, B and C)

> Therefore all creation yearns with eager longing
> as angels and archangels sing the endless hymn of praise...
> (Pentecost Extended Preface)

The preface leads into the *Sanctus*, the Latin for 'holy', which is usually followed by the *Benedictus*, the Latin for 'blessed'. These are congregational texts, sung or said, and both are discussed in Chapter 6.

After the preface the Eucharistic Prayer moves forward with a prayer for the Holy Spirit to touch the bread and wine in such a way as to make them for us the body and blood of Christ. The Greek for this invoking of the Spirit (as explained on page xv) is *epiclesis*, which means literally a 'calling upon' and refers to the calling on the Spirit to act. As a result, *epiclesis* has become a technical term for this part of the prayer. The wording of the *epiclesis* varies from prayer to prayer, sometimes very clearly relating to the elements of bread and wine, as in Prayer A:

> grant that by the power of your Holy Spirit
> these gifts of bread and wine
> may be to us his body and his blood

but sometimes apparently more directed to the communicants as in Prayer C:

> grant that, by the power of your Holy Spirit,
> we receiving these gifts of your creation, this bread and this wine,
> according to your Son our Saviour Jesus Christ's holy institution,
> in remembrance of his death and passion,
> may be partakers of his most blessed body and blood . . .

In the Eastern churches the *epiclesis* has long been regarded as a moment of consecration, but in the West the focus moved to the words of institution and the *epiclesis* disappeared or became so nuanced as to be invisible. Thus in the Book of Common Prayer at this point the Spirit is not mentioned. But contemporary Eucharistic Prayers have all restored an explicit *epiclesis*, though there are differing views about its place in the prayer, discussed below.

In the classic Western shape of the prayer, the *epiclesis* leads into the narrative of the institution. There is an Anglican text, almost unchanged from Thomas Cranmer's First Prayer Book of 1549, found now in the majority of the Eucharistic Prayers of *Common Worship*, and there are variants of text in others of the prayers. These are discussed in Chapter 8. The words spoken by Jesus at the last supper, normally called the 'words of institution', are sometimes also referred to as 'the words of consecration'. But that, of course, depends on a particular theology of the prayer that focuses the transforming action of God on the repetition of those particular words. It is the theology that has been dominant in the West, is reflected in all the prayers of the Roman rite and is well established in the devotional understanding of many churchgoers, certainly in the more Catholic tradition, where the words are accompanied by elevations of the bread and the cup and by the ringing of bells. The scholars, however, tend to play down the consecratory role of the narrative of institution, preferring either to lay emphasis on the *epiclesis* or on the consecratory nature of the whole prayer from beginning to end.

Next comes one of a set of 'memorial acclamations', though in some of the prayers their appearance is delayed for a further paragraph. These form a modern congregational element in the prayer. They prefigure or echo the words in this part of the prayer relating to the death and resurrection of Jesus and his coming in glory. The acclamations do not themselves have a distinct theological function, rather they simply increase the vocal participation of the community. We discuss them in Chapter 6.

Even if a memorial acclamation intervenes, the Eucharistic Prayer moves swiftly from the narrative of the institution into a recalling of the mighty acts of God in the death, resurrection and ascension of Jesus, and looks towards the second coming. This section of the prayer is usually known by the Greek word *anamnesis* (first mentioned on page xv), literally 'remembering', but the translation is inadequate. The English concept of 'remembering' is much weaker than what is meant by the Greek. The Greek word also draws on a Hebrew background and came to mean a sense of remembering with such intensity that the past is made present. At this point of the prayer, we do not just remember a moment in history but live that moment again each time the words of institution are said.

The words of institution bring into our mind Maundy Thursday and the supper in the upper room. The *anamnesis* moves our mind on to Good Friday, to Easter morning and to the ascension, and adds, to complete the picture, a looking forward to Christ's coming again. The verbs employed in this section of the prayer are significant. Catholic liturgy has usually wanted to place alongside 'remembering' the concept of 'offering'. 'Offering' the bread and the cup is, however, a thought that has seemed to many Anglicans to imply a medieval understanding of the Mass as a sacrifice, repeating in a sense the sacrifice of Jesus on the cross, so the hunt has been on for words that express what the Church is doing in the Eucharist without using the language of offering, or indeed of sacrifice unless it be a 'sacrifice of praise and thanksgiving', which was Thomas Cranmer's phrase used *after* Communion. So this is doctrinally a sensitive part of the prayer where every word has been weighed. (In some of the prayers it is only after this *anamnesis* paragraph that the memorial acclamations are used, and this has logic for they are, to a great extent, a recapitulation of that paragraph.)

The *anamnesis* leads into a prayer for and about the participants. It is a prayer that their reception of the consecrated bread and wine may be fruitful in changing and shaping their lives. There is a hope expressed variously that the sacrament will strengthen their sense of being the body of Christ, that they may be renewed, inspired and united, that they may work effectively to see God's kingdom and that they may come to share with the saints in the life of heaven.

In the classic Western shape, this part of the prayer includes a second *epiclesis*. A prayer for fruitful reception becomes, much more specifically, a prayer that the Holy Spirit will come upon the people, just as the Spirit has come upon the bread and wine. This is seen most clearly in Eucharistic Prayer B and is discussed in Chapter 10. But contemporary Eucharistic Prayers have tried to return to the Eastern practice of one *epiclesis* at this late point in the prayer, rejecting the idea of the institution narrative as consecratory and regarding this prayer for the Spirit to come simultaneously on the elements and on the people as a more satisfactory way theologically and liturgically. In the Church of England this was first proposed in the Prayer Book of 1927/8, which Parliament rejected as much as anything because of catholic suspicion of just this innovation. But thinking has moved on and in *Common Worship* both Eucharistic Prayer F and G follow this shape. This is the one significant variation in shape referred to above.

In 1549 the Eucharistic Prayer included a major element of intercession. In a modified form that omits prayer for the departed and commemoration of the saints, it is the prayer 'for the whole state of Christ's Church militant here in earth' in the 1662 Prayer Book. In 1662 it stands alone, separated from the prayer of consecration by the prayers of penitence and other material. But in 1549 it was at the heart of the Eucharistic Prayer, between the *Sanctus* and the consecration. By 1552 it had been removed to its earlier place in the rite so that intercession within the Eucharistic Prayer should not be taken to support a doctrine of the offering of the Mass for particular intentions. From that time for nearly 450 years, intercession formed no part of the Eucharistic Prayer in the Church of England, but *Common Worship* restores the possibility in Prayers F and G.

All that remains is to bring the prayer to its end and its climax, sometimes by reference to the worship of heaven and the lives of the saints, always by affirming that the prayer is offered 'through Jesus Christ', always leading into a prayer of praise, a 'doxology', celebrating the mystery of the Trinity, always in words such as this (from Prayers B and F):

by whom, and with whom, and in whom,
in the unity of the Holy Spirit,
all honour and glory be yours, almighty Father,
for ever and ever.
Amen.

The 'Amen' is important, for just as the prayer has begun with a dialogue that indicates the assent of the community, so it ends with a bold 'Amen' by which the participants make the prayer their own and identify themselves with it. Prayer H in *Common Worship* has rightly been criticized for its omission. Three of the *Common Worship* prayers (A, D and G) give the congregation a longer vocal response, drawing on Revelation 5.13:

**Blessing and honour and glory and power
be yours for ever and ever.
Amen.**

The 'Amen' here is still the crucial word of assent. In saying it the congregation is affirming its agreement with everything that has come before it.

6

The common texts of the Eucharistic Prayer

For all their variety, the Eucharistic Prayers of *Common Worship* have some common texts and share these with the eucharistic rites of other provinces and churches. These are an opening dialogue, a song usually called by its Latin name, *Sanctus*, nearly always joined to a further text, *Benedictus*, and a set of four 'memorial acclamations'.

The Lord be with you
and also with you.

(or)

The Lord is here.
His Spirit is with us.

Lift up your hearts.
We lift them to the Lord.

Let us give thanks to the Lord our God.
It is right to give thanks and praise.

The Eucharistic Prayer begins with a dialogue between the president and the rest of the people present. Historically it was called the *Sursum Corda*, which, as has been said, is simply the Latin text of the third line, 'Lift up your hearts'. This dialogue has a long and unbroken history that can be traced back as far as the early third-century *Apostolic Tradition* of Hippolytus.

The dialogue is important because, right at the start of the prayer, it sets up a relationship between people and president, and makes clear that they offer the prayer together. While the president is the spokesperson, everyone present declares that they agree not only that they will lift up their hearts and give thanks, but that it is right to do this. In this set-piece conversation, the people urge the president on as he or she begins to pray this most important prayer. Although they fall silent for a while after this dialogue, they join in again with an 'Amen' when the prayer ends. By doing so they are agreeing with everything the president has said up to that point and reminding themselves again that the president was articulating their prayers.

For some people it is also important to identify, right at the beginning of the prayer, the role of the Holy Spirit in what is to happen. One of the key questions in this dialogue is who 'the Lord' is in the first line. This is often, also, one of the challenges of the New Testament. The problem is that in the Old Testament 'the Lord' referred to God. Indeed whenever in Hebrew the name for God (YHWH) appeared, Jews said, and still say, '*Adonai*' instead, which is Hebrew for 'Lord'. In the New Testament, then, using 'Lord' to refer to Jesus was saying something deeply important about who the early Christians thought Jesus was (as well as challenging the Roman Empire and its claim that the emperor was the lord). When we get to the creed the use has moved on even further, since there we say, 'the Lord, the giver of life', referring to the Holy Spirit.

Of course, this throws up the question of who the Lord is in the opening sentence of the dialogue. When the president expresses the wish that the Lord might be with the people, who is being referred to? God the Father? God the Son? God the Holy Spirit? Or all three?

It is, to put it mildly, slightly confusing that the answer to this question is not all that clear. In the exchange, 'The Lord be with you' 'and also with you', the majority of scholars have concluded that the 'Lord' referred to here is in fact the Holy Spirit. Indeed the exchange seems to draw deeply on Romans 8.16. In the original Latin version of this dialogue, the response to the greeting ('The Lord be with you') is, literally, 'and with your spirit' (and it is interesting that the latest translation of the Roman Mass has returned to that translation). The 'spirit' in the second phrase is not the Holy Spirit but the spirit of the individual, the very being of each person. The original form of this greeting, then, is acknowledging the point that Paul made in Romans 8.16 (and indeed throughout the whole passage of 8.14–27), where he notes the importance of the link between the Holy Spirit and our own spirits. The presence of the Holy Spirit is precisely to be encountered in each one of our spirits.

The confusion of meaning may well explain why so much interest has centred on these first two lines of the dialogue. In Thomas Cranmer's First Prayer Book these first two lines are preserved, but by the Second Prayer Book they have been removed. There is no agreement, however, as to why they were removed. Cranmer evidently saw some kind of problem with this exchange, but there is little agreement about what this problem might have been.

In the twentieth century, there was an attempt to commend a paraphrase, thought to bring out more clearly the meaning of the original. 'Series 3' substituted for the traditional text the words 'The Lord is here', with its response: 'His Spirit is with us.' The reason for this is that, in the original Latin, there is no verb (so it reads literally, 'The Lord with you'). As a result, this could be as easily a statement as a greeting. The alternative then is exactly that, a statement, not a greeting, with the particular aim of making the reference to the Holy Spirit explicit. The problem is that it confuses even more who the Lord is. In the alternative, 'the Lord' is not the Holy Spirit, because otherwise it would be impossible to declare that his Spirit is with us. So 'the Lord', here, must be God the Father or God the Son.

Subsequent revisions have restored the traditional form, alongside the novel paraphrase, and *Common Worship* always prints the traditional form first. The Liturgical Commission wanted to omit the alternative in 2000, believing that the relational exchange in greeting form was what was required at the beginning of the dialogue and that the paraphrase was an eccentricity that put the Church of England out of line with ecumenical texts, but the paraphrase had so established itself in some communities during the previous 30 years that the Commission bowed to pressure to retain it as an option, though not one for which it had any enthusiasm.

The opening two lines of the dialogue do not quote directly any part of Scripture, but the phrase 'The Lord be with you' obviously has rich resonance with the biblical desire for God to dwell in the midst of his people. Probably the most important expression of this desire can be found in Isaiah 7.14, where the name of the child born of a young woman was declared to be 'Immanuel' or 'God is with us'. This strand, picked up particularly by Matthew, and referring now to Jesus, reminds us of the importance of God's presence in the midst of his people in the Judaeo-Christian tradition.

The third line of the dialogue comes almost directly from Lamentations 3.41 ('Let us lift up our hearts as well as our hands to God in heaven') and makes much more sense of the command to lift up our hearts. As it stands the command seems a little odd: to where should we lift up our hearts? But the Lamentations passage reminds us, first, that the lifting refers to the traditional belief that God dwelt in heaven directly above the earth and that lifting our hearts means directing them to God. Probably even more importantly, though, the point of lifting our hearts is that it refers to the whole of our being. References in the Psalms suggest that the ancient Jewish posture for prayer was standing with hands raised (Psalm 28.2: 'Hear the voice of my supplication, as I cry to you for help, as I lift up my hands towards your most holy sanctuary' or Psalm 63.4: 'So I will bless you as long as I live; I will lift up my hands and call on your name'). The verse from Lamentations is a reminder that posture is not everything in prayer. Much more important is inner attitude and that when we pray we direct the whole of our being towards God.

Lines five and six complete the progression of ideas in the dialogue. We begin with acknowledging the importance of the presence of the Holy Spirit; such a presence causes us to lift the whole of our being, and not just our hands, to God. Once we have done so, the only right course of action is to give thanks. One of the themes that emerges over and over again in the Old Testament is that the only suitable response to God, and who he is, is thanksgiving. The recognition of the deep nature of God and all he has done for us naturally draws from us expressions of thanksgiving and praise; hence the acknowledgement by the people in the dialogue that this is the appropriate response to God.

While the sentiment of line six is clear, it has, like lines one and two, received considerable attention. The phrase 'It is right to give thanks and praise' has no object in the original Latin, nor indeed has Cranmer's translation of it: 'It is meet and right so to do.' But 'Series 3' rendered this line 'It is right to give *him* thanks and praise' (emphasis added). At the time this seemed unexceptionable, but with a growing awareness of gender-inclusive language for God as much as for human beings, 'him' became less acceptable, some congregations saying instead, 'our thanks and praise', others 'God thanks and praise.' *Common Worship* opted to return to the original and omit an object altogether.

Whatever the detail, the function of this dialogue, having established relationship and authority, is to build the prayer up so that, when the president takes off into the words of the preface, it is from a high point of engagement and expectation, carrying the people along as the prayer develops.

At the conclusion of that preface, which varies from Eucharistic Prayer to Eucharistic Prayer and from one season to another, comes this song:

> Holy, holy, holy Lord,
> God of power and might,
> heaven and earth are full of your glory.
> Hosanna in the highest.
> [Blessed is he who comes in the name of the Lord.
> Hosanna in the highest.]

The first four lines constitute the *Sanctus*, the fifth and sixth lines the *Benedictus*, both from the first word in the Latin, 'holy' and 'blessed'. Although the earliest usage of the *Sanctus* was without the *Benedictus*, the *Benedictus* became added quite early on and now the two texts usually belong together. There is uncertainty about the origin of this song, but by the fourth century it is established in the eucharistic liturgies of Antioch, Jerusalem and Egypt and, by the sixth century, of Rome also. Only one ancient liturgy omits it altogether, and it has been regarded as an essential part of the Eucharistic Prayer.

Archbishop Cranmer included it in 1549, though he changed the second 'Hosanna in the highest' to 'Glory to thee, O Lord, in the highest.' This may simply have been due to his dislike of any word that was not straightforwardly English. 'Hosanna' perhaps had to go, just as 'Alleluia' disappeared also. Certainly by the time of his 1552 Book, 'Hosanna' has quite disappeared. But then so has the whole of the *Benedictus*, and here the issue was not just about language but also about doctrine. To sing 'Blessed is he that cometh in the name of the Lord' just before consecrating the bread and wine was beginning to be seen as introducing an unacceptable doctrine that a change was about to happen whereby the Lord would come in response to words of consecration. So Cranmer removed them. Subsequent revision of the liturgy has brought them back, but not always to their traditional place. *Holy Communion Second Series* put them at the end of the Eucharistic Prayer, for which there was some historical precedent. 'Series 3' put them during the distribution. *ASB* restored them to their place with the *Sanctus*, but with the possibility of their omission. In most churches today they are used where they are printed: back in their traditional place.

The function of the *Sanctus* and *Benedictus* is to enable all those present to respond orally to the preface, which has just been prayed by the president. The preface is a prayer that brings together remembering and praising (see Chapter 7 for more on the prefaces), and culminates in the words of the

Sanctus and *Benedictus* through which all the members of the congregation join their thanksgiving with the praises of the angels and saints around God's throne. The words of the *Sanctus* join the Church on earth with 'all the company of heaven' in words the Scriptures associate with the angels. The 'Blessed is he' is an extension of that and calls to mind the one who comes in God's name from that heavenly place to share our life on earth.

The song 'Holy, holy, holy' is the song sung by the seraphim before God's throne in Isaiah 6. In this vision, Isaiah caught sight of God's enormous heavenly throne that spanned heaven and earth, a throne that was so big that the very hem of his robe filled the Temple. On this occasion Isaiah was given insight into the songs that the angels (here the seraphim) sing before God's throne day and night. In the words of the *Sanctus*, then, we are invited to join in with the songs of the angels before God's throne. It is a moment when the veil between heaven and earth is drawn aside and we are drawn into the worship of heaven. The words of the *Sanctus* change the words of Isaiah 6.3 slightly in order to remind us of this. In 6.3 the seraphim sang that '*the whole earth* is full of [God's] glory' (emphasis added). The *Sanctus* changes this to 'heaven and earth' to remind us that the two are joined as we sing this song.

The third line of the *Sanctus* – 'Hosanna in the highest' – is really a misplaced line from the *Benedictus*. This line had been added to the *Sanctus* in the East by the fifth century (where it is found in the Liturgy of St James) and in the West by the eighth century.

The word 'Hosanna' is so commonly used in Christian worship that it comes as something of a surprise to discover that it occurs only once in the Old Testament, in Psalm 118.25, and in the New Testament when Psalm 118.25–26 is quoted at Jesus' triumphal entry into Jerusalem. It is not originally an exclamation of praise but a plea for help. Indeed if we look up Psalm 118.25 in our English Old Testaments we won't find the word 'Hosanna' at all. Instead we will find the English phrase, 'Save us, we beseech you' (this is what the word actually means – 'save us now'). Over time, people became so confident that God would save them that it became an expression of anticipatory praise. So certain were they that God would save them that the plea for salvation became tinged with the knowledge that he always would.

Psalm 118 was originally a psalm that gave thanks to God for saving one of the 'kings of David' from disaster. By the time of Jesus it had become a psalm that was used to speak of the hopes of the people of Israel as they waited for a new Davidic king to come and save them. It was also one of the psalms that would have been sung by pilgrims on their way to the Temple. Its use when Jesus entered Jerusalem was to be expected because the people were all on their way to the Temple for Passover, but it gained in significance because Jesus was, of course, the Davidic leader for whom they waited.

It is the Gospel versions of this psalm that introduce the words 'in the highest heaven' (see for example Matthew 21.9). It is a phrase that points to the plea for salvation rising before God's throne in heaven, and our assurance that God will hear that plea.

The combination of the *Sanctus* with the *Benedictus* explicitly joins the song of heaven ('Holy, holy, holy') with the song of earth ('Hosanna'), and reminds us that in the Eucharist heaven and earth are joined in their praise of God: we do not worship alone but join with those whose worship of God never ceases.

A little later come 'the memorial acclamations', as they are called in the Roman Mass from which they are derived.

[Great is the mystery of faith:]
Christ has died:
Christ is risen:
Christ will come again.

[Praise to you, Lord Jesus:]
Dying you destroyed our death,
rising you restored our life:
Lord Jesus, come in glory.

[Christ is the bread of life:]
When we eat this bread and drink this cup,
we proclaim your death, Lord Jesus,
until you come in glory.

[Jesus Christ is Lord:]
Lord, by your cross and resurrection
you have set us free.
You are the Saviour of the world.

Although these acclamations sound scriptural, they are more paraphrases than quotations, drawing ideas from around the New Testament. Each one is a distillation of key beliefs about the last supper or Jesus' death, resurrection and second coming. The closest to a quotation is the third acclamation, which picks up Paul's words in 1 Corinthians 11.26: 'For as often as you eat this bread and drink the cup, you proclaim the Lord's death until he comes.'

The rest are poetic summaries of theology drawn from various different places in the New Testament. The first and most commonly used acclamation draws together the simple facts of Jesus' death, resurrection and second coming, but in doing so gives weight to the belief about the second coming. The first two have happened; the third will happen. Our assurance about Jesus' return is given by our knowledge that he has died and is risen. The first two lend us confidence in the third acclamation.

The second acclamation is like the first (the death and resurrection offer us confidence that Jesus' return will happen), with an additional – and crucial – theological element. The importance of Jesus' death and resurrection is not just that they happened to him but that, as a result, our lives have changed too. Drawing on passages like 1 Corinthians 15.26 and Hebrews 2.14, the first phrase, 'Dying you destroyed our death', reminds us that Jesus' own death so changed the world that death – as in eternal death – and its power have been destroyed. As a result of this, Jesus' resurrection has restored fullness of life (e.g. Romans 6.4). Our confidence in the destruction of eternal death and the restoration of true life is what allows us to join in with the earliest Christians to pray, '*Maranatha*', which is Aramaic for 'Come, Lord' and is widely believed to be one of the earliest prayers of the Christian community.

The fourth acclamation focuses less on our future hope and more on what Christ has done. This acclamation reminds us that Jesus' death freed us from slavery to sin and his resurrection freed us for new life in Christ, and that this salvation is a salvation available to the whole world.

Again, although some of their phrases have long been in the liturgy, memorial acclamations are a twentieth-century device as far as the Church in the West is concerned, designed to make more active and oral the participation of the people in the Eucharistic Prayer, guarding against it becoming a presidential monologue.

Although such acclamations were pioneered by the liturgy of the Church of South India in 1958, these memorial acclamations appeared for the first time in the post-Vatican Council translations of the Roman Mass. In their different ways they enable the community to focus on the death and resurrection of Jesus, and three out of the four add reference to his second coming. Because they are responses to the recalling of his death and resurrection, the most logical place for them is after the *anamnesis* (the words the president speaks after the words of institution about the cross and resurrection), but, not entirely satisfactorily, they first found a place immediately after the words of institution, highlighting those words as particularly significant. In *Common Worship* some of the Eucharistic Prayers (B, C, G) place the acclamations immediately after the words of institution, some (A, E) after the *anamnesis*, and others (D, F, H) omit them altogether.

The most traditional of the acclamations, and perhaps the most satisfactory, is the second. It is found in Palestinian and Egyptian liturgies. But the first one to be introduced into the Church of England was 'Christ has died . . .' and, because of its priority, it is the most established. There is an interesting element to its introduction in the General Synod, where the Liturgical Commission originally provided as the third line, 'In Christ shall all be made alive', but under pressure this was later conformed to the Roman text. Also, at a later date, came the cue line 'Great is the mystery of faith', over which people have sometimes puzzled. The traditional Roman rite included the words 'this is the cup of my blood, of the new and eternal covenant, the mystery of faith, which will be shed for you.' Removing the phrase 'the mystery of faith' from the text of the institution narrative, the Roman revisers turned it into an introduction to the acclamations – changing the meaning, in so doing, to include the whole work of redemption.

It is worth mentioning, in conclusion, the great 'Amen' with which the Eucharistic Prayer ends. Sometimes sung, sometimes repeated, sometimes concluding a final acclamation, it signifies the assent of the community. Indeed the word 'Amen' is an interesting one in the Bible. It is probably Hebrew in origin – though a similar form also occurs in other Semitic languages – and is the participle of the verb *aman*, which has resonances of 'to support', 'to be faithful', 'to confirm', 'to be reliable'. As a result 'Amen' means something along the lines of 'What has just been said is reliable.' It is in effect the liturgical equivalent of signing your name at the end of a document to show you agree. This is certainly the case in most of the Bible where 'Amen' is used to agree to things either said by someone else (e.g. 1 Kings 1.36) or to confirm something that has been said corporately. The only exception to this is Jesus' use of the double 'Amen, Amen' at the start of a number of his sayings (e.g. John 1.51) to mark the seriousness of what he is about to say. 'Amen' is never used like this anywhere else. Here in the service the word offers the congregation the opportunity to make the words said by the president their own.

Just as the opening dialogue has indicated consent at the beginning of the prayer, so this response to the doxology confirms that this is the thanksgiving prayer of the whole community. In *Common Worship* the 'Amen' in Prayers A and G is preceded by 'Blessing and honour and glory and power be yours for ever and ever.' But the last word remains 'Amen.'

7

Proper prefaces

The 'proper preface' is the variable part of the Eucharistic Prayer before the *Sanctus*. Such prefaces are unknown in the Eastern churches, where each Eucharistic Prayer has its own invariable preface. That is also the case in *Common Worship* in relation to Prayers D, F, G and H, reflecting Eastern practice. But the norm in the West has been to use variable prefaces that highlight the particular season, saint or mystery being celebrated on a particular day.

Thomas Cranmer in 1549 reduced the number of such prefaces to five, jettisoning the other pre-Reformation texts, most of which came from the Sarum Missal, which was the dominant eucharistic book in use in England in medieval times. These five, for Christmas Day, Easter Day, Ascension, Whitsunday and Trinity Sunday, were to be used only on those five feast days. On 360 days of the year there was to be no proper preface. The Eucharist moved from the dialogue to the *Sanctus* in the briefest of texts, with no mention of Christ and no telling of the drama of salvation.

> It is very meet, right and our bounden duty, that we should at all times, and in all places, give thanks unto thee, O Lord holy Father, almighty and everlasting God. Therefore with Angels and Archangels, and with all the company of heaven, we laud and magnify thy glorious name, evermore praising thee, and saying . . .

Even the 1552 Prayer Book, which in general reduced liturgical provision, increased the use of these prefaces to include the seven days after Christmas, Easter and Ascension and the six days after Pentecost. The 1662 book made no change; 1928 and 'Series 1' increased the number. 'Series 2' introduced a longer regular preface and reduced the number of proper prefaces again. With 'Series 3' the number once again increased, and *ASB* and *Common Worship* have both added more. *ASB* introduced the idea of omitting most, though not all, of the longer regular or 'common' preface where a proper preface is to be inserted, and this remains the case in Eucharistic Prayer A. *Common Worship* has gone a stage further and requires, in relation to Prayers A, B and E, the omission of the entire common preface if an 'extended' proper preface is to be used.

The point of the prefaces is to rehearse and remind all those present – president and congregation – of why it is they have gathered to give thanks. The real value of the seasonal prefaces is that it is possible to highlight different emphases in our thanksgiving at different times of the year. So at Christmas we give thanks for the Incarnation, at Easter for the resurrection, and so on.

The prefaces in *Common Worship* are legion and it would be quite impossible to explore all of them here without doubling the size of this book. But in order to explore the way they use biblical imagery, we have chosen to look at the five that Cranmer included in 1549 and 1552 and see how they have been modified, and also to examine the (potentially) most commonly used proper prefaces in *Common Worship*: those for the Sundays of Ordinary Time.

Cranmer's preface for Christmas Day and the seven days after is

> because thou didst give Jesus Christ thine only Son to be born as at this time for us; who, by the operation of the Holy Ghost, was made very man of the substance of the Virgin Mary his mother; and that without spot of sin, to make us clean from all sin.

Common Worship has made a number of changes, but it is recognizable as the same basic set of truths. Its use is permitted until Epiphany.

In each of these prefaces it is interesting to observe what the key themes of each season are perceived to be. The Christmas preface joins the basic facts of Jesus' birth – that he was conceived by the Holy Spirit, that he was fully human and that his mother, Mary, was a virgin such as can be found in Luke 1.34–35 – with the theme from both Paul and Hebrews of the sinlessness of Jesus that made it possible for him to cleanse us from sin (e.g. 2 Corinthians 5.21; Hebrews 4.15). As a result, though we might expect the Christmas preface to be focused solely on the Incarnation, we find instead a dual focus on incarnation and salvation:

> because, by the power of the Holy Spirit,
> he took our nature upon him
> and was born of the Virgin Mary his mother,
> that being himself without sin,
> he might make us clean from all sin.

The Eastertide preface in *Common Worship* is so like Cranmer's preface for Easter Day and the seven days after that it is not necessary to print the earlier version for comparison. *Common Worship* has

> But chiefly are we bound to praise you
> because you raised him gloriously from the dead.
> For he is the true paschal lamb who was offered for us,
> and has taken away the sin of the world.
> By his death he has destroyed death,
> and by his rising to life again he has restored to us
>   everlasting life.

Just as the Christmastide preface reminds us that the Incarnation has woven within it Jesus' ultimate act of salvation to cleanse our sin, so the Eastertide preface reminds us that we cannot have resurrection without death. The two are two sides of the same coin: Jesus' death has destroyed death and Jesus' resurrection has restored life. Death and life are bound together and cannot be disentangled. This theme of Jesus' death as being

a victory over death comes in various places both in Paul and
Hebrews (e.g. 1 Corinthians 15.26 and Hebrews 2.14). Somewhat
intriguingly, the preface introduces a second key theological
point into the middle of the preface. While the first two lines
and the last two lines of the preface weave together death and
resurrection, the middle two lines introduce an entirely different, Johannine, image: that of Jesus as the paschal lamb who
takes away the sin of the world.

Similarly, with the ascension (*Common Worship*, like 1549,
orders this preface only on the feast itself), the current text is
simply a contemporary version of the older text:

> because, after his most glorious resurrection,
> he appeared to his disciples,
> and in their sight ascended into heaven to prepare a place for us;
> that where he is, thither we might also ascend,
> and reign with him in glory.

Unlike the Christmas and Easter prefaces, the Ascension preface keeps the focus on a single event: the ascension and its
impact on the lives of Christians and, although the preface
could have introduced the theme of Jesus taking humanity
into the heart of the Godhead and interceding for us there,
it does not. Instead it picks up the Johannine theme of
Jesus going ahead of us to prepare a place for us (John 14.2–3)
and seems to connect this with a belief that after death we
too will ascend to heaven to reign with Christ. While the
notion of co-reigning with Christ is clearly from the New
Testament (e.g. 2 Timothy 2.12), the notion that this will
happen in *heaven* is harder to argue. Indeed it seems more
likely that this reigning with Christ will take place in God's
kingdom on earth (e.g. Luke 22.28–30) after Christ has come
in glory.

But 1662 and *Common Worship* handle the preface for Pentecost differently from one another. Cranmer's text, as set out
in 1552 and 1662 for Whitsunday and the six days after, reads:

Through Jesus Christ our Lord; according to whose most true promise, the Holy Ghost came down as at this time from heaven with a sudden great sound, as it had been a mighty wind, in the likeness of fiery tongues, lighting upon the Apostles, to teach them, and to lead them to all truth; giving them both the gift of divers languages, and also boldness with fervent zeal constantly to preach the gospel unto all nations; whereby we have been brought out of darkness and error into the clear light and true knowledge of thee, and of thy Son Jesus Christ.

This is a different approach, a retelling of the story, almost word for word from Acts 2, which will already have been read in the Eucharist on Whitsunday itself. It is an approach favoured by some of the new extended prefaces that also adopt this biblical narrative approach. But from 1928 it was thought too repetitive of the reading from Acts and was replaced with a preface that is the antecedent of that for Pentecost in *Common Worship*:

> And now we give you thanks
> that, after he had ascended far above all heavens,
> and was seated at the right hand of your majesty,
> he sent forth upon the universal Church your holy and life-giving
>   Spirit;
> that through his glorious power the joy of the everlasting gospel
>   might go forth into all the world.

Although not so close to the text of Acts 2, this passage could be said to summarize the whole of the Acts of the Apostles. From the ascension mentioned in chapter 1 to the sending of the Spirit in chapter 2, the ending of the preface points our attention to the spreading of the good news of Jesus Christ to the end of the earth. An important phrase in this preface is 'holy and life-giving Spirit'. We are used to 'the Holy Spirit' being used as a title for the Spirit but this additional element, 'life-giving' (or, as would be closer to the Greek, 'life-making') is also important. On a number of occasions both John and Paul associate life-making with the Spirit (e.g. John 6.63;

1 Corinthians 15.45; 2 Corinthians 3.6). This is important. The Spirit is not just holy but is also life-generating. If we want to discern the presence of the Spirit, we need to look for signs of life.

Trinity Sunday in the old rites required the omission of the words 'holy Father' from the common text, so that the preface might be addressed to all three persons of the Trinity. Thus:

> Who art one God, one Lord; not only one person, but three persons in one substance. For that which we believe of the glory of the Father, the same we believe of the Son, and of the Holy Ghost, without any difference or inequality.

The *Common Worship* preface for the day, addressed to the Father, is clearly derived from it, but is less didactic and more doxological.

> because you have revealed the glory of your eternal fellowship
>> of love with your Son and with the Holy Spirit,
> three persons, equal in majesty, undivided in splendour,
> yet one God,
> ever to be worshipped and adored.

The emphases of this preface are, appropriately, post-biblical given the theme of the Trinity. Although the Trinity features in the Bible on numerous key occasions (e.g. Matthew 28.19; 2 Corinthians 13.13; Galatians 4.6), the finely honed statements about the nature of the Trinity, one God in three persons, belong to centuries after the writing of the New Testament.

After the Reformation there was no proper preface for Sundays until 1928, where a preface was provided that is now a default option – when there is no other proper preface – in *Common Worship* Eucharistic Prayer C. There was no Sunday preface in 'Series 2' or 'Series 3'. *ASB* provided three such prefaces, but restricted their use to Eucharistic Prayer 4, though it is difficult to see why. Unchanged, but no longer restricted to one prayer, and available for use with Prayers A, B and C, they emphasize the three events associated with the first day of the week: Creation, resurrection and the coming of the Spirit. Each one draws on a key feature of the nature of the Trinity and shows how this feature affects the lives of God's people (he calls us to new life, e.g. 1 Peter 1.3; has opened the way of everlasting life, e.g. Romans 6.4; and has made us a new people, 1 Peter 2.9).

> And now we give you thanks
> because you are the source of light and life;
> you made us in your image
> and called us to new life in him.

> And now we give you thanks
> because on the first day of the week
> he overcame death and the grave
> and opened to us the way of everlasting life.

> And now we give you thanks
> because by water and the Holy Spirit
> you have made us in him a new people to show forth your glory.

The final text is an example of *Common Worship*'s extended prefaces for use with Prayers A, B and E, this one for Sundays in Ordinary Time. The source, as with several others of the extended prefaces, is the new Roman Catholic Sacramentary. It weaves together the themes of light and darkness with the evocative story of the road to Emmaus. The mention of sunrise to sunset and the scattering of darkness brings to mind the theme of Creation which, when coupled with the resurrection, reminds us that in the Eucharist we celebrate the way in which time collapses in on itself so that at one and the same time we celebrate the old *and* the new Creation: God's first bringing of life with his bringing to new life in Jesus' resurrection, and not only that – we also celebrate the fact that just as Jesus walked with the disciples to Emmaus, so also he walks with us in our lives. In the Eucharist we stand in a swirl of time in which the first Creation, the new life of Christ at the resurrection, the ongoing walking of Christ alongside us in our own lives and the ultimate recreation of all things collide, become present and are celebrated. This beautiful preface seeks through its poetic language to remind us of this.

It is truly right and just, our duty and our salvation,
always and everywhere to give you thanks,
holy Father, almighty and eternal God.
From sunrise to sunset this day is holy,
for Christ has risen from the tomb
and scattered the darkness of death
with light that will not fade.
This day the risen Lord walks with your gathered people,
unfolds for us your word,
and makes himself known in the breaking of bread.
And though the night will overtake this day
you summon us to live in endless light,
the never-ceasing sabbath of the Lord.
And so, with choirs of angels
and with all the heavenly host,
we proclaim your glory
and join their unending song of praise.

8

The institution narrative

The narrative of the institution of the Eucharist at the 'last supper' has always been seen as a crucial part of eucharistic liturgy. There is only one known exception and that is the third-century Syrian liturgy of Addai and Mari which, in a Eucharistic Prayer addressed to Jesus, rather than to the Father, does not employ the words of Jesus at the last supper. Some Protestant churches have viewed 1 Corinthians 11.23–25 as a 'scriptural warrant', being content to read an account, rather than to offer a prayer that includes the words that Jesus used. But otherwise the near universal practice of the Church has been to turn the biblical account into a prayer, addressed to the Father, and to regard it as a non-negotiable part of the Eucharistic Prayer, included for at least four reasons. The first is that the narrative set the meal within its historical context of the night before Jesus died. The second is that it gave the warrant for the celebration by spelling out his command: 'Do this . . . in remembrance of me' (v. 25). Third, it affirmed that the bread and wine became for the Church the body and blood of Christ in accordance with the words of Jesus himself. Finally, it employed language that drew out of the worshippers thanksgiving for Christ's unique work of saving humankind by his death on the cross.

To these four reasons can be added, for some churches and at some points in liturgical history, a deeper reason, namely that it was the very words of Jesus, repeated by the priest, that consecrated the bread and wine and made them – however it was exactly understood – the body and blood of the Lord. This is the theology that Cranmer inherited from the Roman rite and, despite his changing attitude to eucharistic doctrine, he does not seem to have moved from a position of seeing the words of Jesus as consecrating the bread and wine to become in some way the body and blood of Jesus Christ.

The institution narrative is not a simple replication of Scripture, partly because it has been turned into prayer, but also from early times the liturgies brought elements of the different accounts, in Matthew, Mark, Luke and Paul (1 Corinthians), together to create a richer and balanced text. In the course of time some liturgies expanded the text to import non-scriptural elements, such as the words in the Roman Eucharistic Prayer that say that Jesus 'took bread in his holy and venerable hands, and with his eyes raised to heaven to you, his almighty Father, gave thanks'.

What Cranmer did do was to strip out the non-biblical accretions and to produce a simple and more streamlined version of the institution narrative. In 1549 he wrote (spelling modernized),

> who in the same night that he was betrayed: took bread, and when he had blessed, and given thanks: he brake it, and gave it to his disciples, saying: Take, eat, this is my body which is given for you, do this in remembrance of me. Likewise after supper he took the cup, and when he had given thanks, he gave it to them saying: drink ye all of this, for this is my blood of the new Testament, which is shed for you and for many, for remission of sins: do this as oft as ye shall drink it, in remembrance of me.

That is the classic English text, for until *Common Worship* the departures from it have been minimal and even in most of the *Common Worship* prayers the words of Jesus remain unchanged.

The 1552 text simply removed the words 'he had blessed, and'; 1662 only added 'the' before 'remission of sins'; 1928 changed 'Testament' to 'Covenant'. 'Series 2' added 'to thee' after 'given thanks', emphasizing the address to the Father, and changed 'brake' to 'broke'.

With the coming of 'Series 3' there was a need for a conservative revision in contemporary English. With little change in *ASB*, this is the form now found in Eucharistic Prayers A, B, C of *Common Worship*.

> who, in the same night that he was betrayed,
> took bread and gave you thanks;
> he broke it and gave it to his disciples, saying:
> Take, eat; this is my body which is given for you;
> do this in remembrance of me.
>
> In the same way, after supper
> he took the cup and gave you thanks;
> he gave it to them, saying:
> Drink this, all of you;
> this is my blood of the new covenant,
> which is shed for you and for many for the forgiveness of sins.
> Do this, as often as you drink it,
> in remembrance of me.

The words of Jesus, the words of institution, are also the same in Eucharistic Prayers E, F and G. Only Prayers D and H are different. H omits the 'and for many'. D says 'my body, given for you all' and 'my blood shed for you all'.

There is slightly greater variety in the way the scene for the supper is set. Prayer D has

> On the night he was betrayed
> he came to table with his friends to celebrate the freedom of
>   your people . . .
> Jesus blessed you, Father, for the food;
> he took bread, gave thanks, broke it and said . . .

Prayer E sets the context in this way:

> On the night before he died he had supper with his friends
> and, taking bread, he praised you.
> He broke the bread, gave it to them and said . . .

Prayer F follows the *Common Worship* norm except for the introductory line, 'On the night he gave up himself for us all'.

G, almost identical to D, has 'came to supper with his friends'. Prayer H has

> On the night he was betrayed,
> at supper with his friends
> he took bread, and gave you thanks ...

These new prayers have in common an emphasis on the fellowship of the meal, with the mention of 'supper' and 'friendship'. There is less emphasis on betrayal and, though in only one prayer, we find the striking phrase, 'gave himself up for us all'.

There was some discussion in the Liturgical Commission about the desirability or otherwise of identical texts at this point in the liturgy. In favour of uniformity is the sense that sacred words go deeper with invariable use and also that this is a point when the president, taking bread and wine into the hands, does not want to be book-bound. Against that is the argument that words can be too familiar, hardly heard because they are used so often, and variations bring greater attention. In the end perhaps the most interesting fact is that the newer versions move us further away from the biblical text. The Gospels have 'Passover meal', rather than 'supper', and 'the twelve' or 'the apostles', rather than 'his friends'.

The other problem is that there is no single unified version of the institution narrative in the Gospels and Paul. The single institution narrative is a harmony of 1 Corinthians 11 with the Gospel accounts, moving from one source to another. For instance, 'Take, eat, this is my body' is drawn from Matthew, but 'Do this in remembrance of me' from 1 Corinthians and Luke. The reference to the cup is a harmonization of all three Gospel accounts with 1 Corinthians.

One major difference between the *Common Worship* texts and the four biblical texts is that the latter all mention a loaf of bread (the Greek word especially refers to a loaf), whereas the liturgical texts all mention just 'bread'.

Probably one of the most overlooked features of the institution narrative is Luke's inclusion of two cups, one before the giving of the bread and one after it. The majority of scholars believe that this takes us back to the Passover meal element of the last supper, where there are four cups (the first for sanctification, the second for deliverance, the third for redemption and the fourth for restoration). Although there is no great agreement among scholars about which of the four each of Luke's two cups refers to, it is at least possible that they fit well with the third and fourth (redemption and restoration).

Given the fact that the other biblical accounts do not mention two cups, it is not surprising that the narrative in the Eucharistic Prayers does not introduce a second cup. In a sense, that illustrates that the Eucharistic Prayers are aiming for something different. The biblical texts retain difference and variety, but the eucharistic texts aim for uniformity, even though that uniformity – embedded in Cranmer's sixteenth-century texts – is stretched to its limit by the multiplicity of Eucharistic Prayers in *Common Worship*. It is to exploration of those Eucharistic Prayers that we now turn.

9

Eucharistic Prayer A

Eucharistic Prayer A, although now one of the eight prayers in *Common Worship* Order One, was in earlier versions the only alternative to a prayer derived from the 1662 rite. In its first version as the Eucharistic Prayer in 'Series 2', it drew considerably on the liturgy of the Church of South India. A number of textual changes as well as a move into contemporary language saw it emerge as the Eucharistic Prayer of 'Series 3'. *ASB* included it in two versions. The First Eucharistic Prayer of Rite A was the direct descendant of the 'Series 3' prayer, with very little textual change. The Second Eucharistic Prayer of Rite A provided a contemporary version of the 'Series 2' prayer, without the 'Series 3' changes but with some new material. The First and Second Eucharistic Prayers were thus quite similar (indeed the preface was identical), and it was perhaps not surprising that those revising the rite for *Common Worship* chose to conflate the two, bringing into the First Eucharistic Prayer some elements of the Second. Eucharistic Prayer A of *Common Worship* is that conflation.

The preface to Eucharistic Prayer A is little changed since 'Series 2', except in a reference to Jesus as 'the living Word' of God. It represents the Church's desire to offer praise at the heart of the Eucharist for the mighty acts of God in Creation, in the resurrection and ascension of Jesus and in the coming of the Spirit, and not simply to focus, as the Book of Common Prayer does, on the saving death of Jesus on the cross.

The text is highly biblical.

> It is indeed right,
> it is our duty and our joy,
> at all times and in all places

to give you thanks and praise,
holy Father, heavenly King,
almighty and eternal God,
through Jesus Christ your Son our Lord.

For he is your living Word;
through him you have created all things from the beginning,
and formed us in your own image.

Through him you have freed us from the slavery of sin,
giving him to be born of a woman and to die upon the cross;
you raised him from the dead
and exalted him to your right hand on high.

Through him you have sent upon us
your holy and life-giving Spirit,
and made us a people for your own possession.

This preface is so rich a theological statement that it is worth going through it phrase by phrase, noting where the different allusions are drawn from and reflecting on their significance.

A phrase of vast importance, which it would be all too easy to miss, is 'through Jesus/him'. This phrase occurs rhythmically four times throughout the preface and draws us back again and again to the centrality of the agency of Jesus Christ. One of the key elements of Paul's theology is that of being 'in Christ'. This is more than just a turn of phrase. Paul believed that those who believed 'in Christ' died and rose with him and, as a result, had a new corporate identity – a Christ identity. This is what allows him to say, 'it is no longer I who live, but it is Christ who lives in me' (Galatians 2.20). The true significance of this is too large to unpack here but, in short, it means that Christ functions as the mediator between God and the world. Our prayer and praise comes to God through Christ, and Christ is the one through whom Creation came into being, through whom liberation from sin is achieved and through whom God's Spirit descends on the world. The fourfold repetition of 'through Jesus/him' serves to remind us of the absolute centrality of Christ in the world, in our lives and in our worship.

The second paragraph of the preface is a rather beautiful conflation of two Christ hymns: John 1.1–14 and Colossians 1.15–20, with some other references thrown in. Both John 1.1–14 and Colossians 1.15–20 reflect, through the lenses both of Genesis 1 and Proverbs 8.22–31, on Christ's agency in Creation. Both stress that all created things found their existence through Jesus Christ, and this is the theme that the preface picks up here. What is added is a reference to Jesus, not just as the Word of God but as the *living* Word, although this could probably be read in from John 1 (the source of all life can hardly be considered to be dead), but may well be drawing on both Hebrews 4.12 and 1 Peter 1.23, which explicitly speaks of God's word as 'living'. In the context it seems clear that both Hebrews and 1 Peter meant God's written word, but it is not a vast step from seeing God's written word as living to seeing Jesus himself as perfectly representing God's living Word on earth.

The next paragraph turns its attention from Creation to salvation (something that also happens in the Colossians hymn). The words 'giving him to be born of a woman and to die upon the cross; you raised him from the dead and exalted him to your right hand on high' all form an expansion of the opening line ('Through him you have freed us from the slavery of sin'). It is easy sometimes to fall into the trap of believing that Christ's death on the cross was the only thing necessary for salvation. It is, of course, the vital piece of the jigsaw, but the jigsaw would be incomplete without the Incarnation, resurrection and ascension. Freedom *from* sin also involves being freed *for* a new life in Christ. If Jesus had just died, we might be freed from sin but there would no freedom into a new future. The new future was shaped through Jesus' resurrection to a new life and continuing life at the right hand of the Father. Thus freedom from sin needs the whole of Jesus' life, death, resurrection and ascension to be effective.

The final paragraph turns our attention to the action of the Spirit, which not only gives us life but in that life makes us God's own people. Although the verbal hints of this are lost between the translation of *Common Worship* and many of the modern English language translations of the New Testament, this draws deeply on 1 Peter 2.9, in which there is a well-known statement about the identity of those who are in Christ: 'you are a chosen race, a royal priesthood, a holy nation, God's own people'. That last phrase, 'God's own people', is more accurately translated 'a people for possession'. In this final paragraph we are reminded that life in Christ is far more than a superficial, rational decision; rather it is something that changes our identity. Through Christ the Spirit has descended on us, transforming us from being 'no people' to being God's own people (see Hosea 1.10).

This identity as the people of God is what makes our engagement with Scripture, both Old and New, so very important. If we are God's own people, it is important to discover where we come from and where we are going. The stories, poems and instructions of the Old and New Testaments give us a family history that defines who we are and gives us a sense of the people we can become in Christ.

In the latter part of the prayer there are three elements that need further exploration. The first is how it handles the language of sacrifice, offering and remembrance. 'Series 3' had

> With this bread and this cup
> we do this in remembrance of him:
> we celebrate and proclaim his perfect sacrifice made once for all upon the cross,
> his resurrection from the dead, and his ascension into heaven;
> and we look for his coming in glory.

The First Eucharistic Prayer of *ASB* stated,

> We remember his offering of himself
> made once for all upon the cross,

and proclaim his mighty resurrection and glorious ascension.
As we look for his coming in glory,
we celebrate with this bread and this cup
his one perfect sacrifice.

The Second Eucharistic Prayer of *ASB* expressed it like this:

Having in remembrance his death once for all upon the cross,
his resurrection from the dead,
and his ascension into heaven,
and looking for the coming of his kingdom,
we make with this bread and this cup
the memorial of Christ your Son our Lord.

In searching for the most satisfactory expression of a doctrinally
sensitive area, Eucharistic Prayer A has settled on

we remember his offering of himself
made once for all upon the cross;
we proclaim his mighty resurrection and glorious ascension;
we look for the coming of your kingdom,
and with this bread and this cup
we make the memorial of Christ your Son our Lord.

Celebrating a sacrifice has given way to making a memorial.

Second, it is worth noting the way the various versions have
spoken of the future, as the texts above reveal. 'Series 3' and
Eucharistic Prayer 1 of *ASB* have 'looking for *his* coming in
glory' (emphasis added). Eucharistic Prayer 2 of *ASB* has 'looking for the coming of his kingdom'. Eucharistic Prayer A has
'we look for the coming of *your* kingdom' (emphasis added).
This change is a good one and more accurately reflects Jesus'
use of language about the kingdom in the Gospels. Although
Matthew more often uses the phrase 'kingdom of heaven' than
'kingdom of God', it is clear that when either phrase is used it
refers to a state in which God rules as King. It is important not
to place too much stress on whose kingdom it is (God's or Jesus'),
but the language of the Gospels makes the default position

clear: the kingdom belongs to God, and Jesus will reign with him from the throne. The change from 'his kingdom' to 'your kingdom' (since the prayer is addressed to God and about Jesus) simply clarifies this small but significant point.

The third issue is simply to note one of the striking innovations of 'Series 3' that has survived all the revisions with its use in the petition for fruitful reception of three strong, memorable phrases:

> renew us by your Spirit,
> inspire us with your love
> and unite us in the body of your Son . . .

This triplet picks up a semi-Trinitarian phrase that appears twice in Paul, once in the much better-known 'Grace' in 2 Corinthians 13.13, and once in Philippians 2.1, where Paul encourages the Philippians to have the mind of Christ, introducing his point with the threefold clause: 'If then there is any encouragement in Christ, any consolation from love, any sharing in the Spirit' (though we should note that after this he adds a fourth formulation, 'any compassion and sympathy' which somewhat undermines the Trinitarian element). In both of these cases 'love' is either explicitly (in 2 Corinthians 13.13) or implicitly (in Philippians 2.1) associated with God, as it appears to be in this prayer too.

Eucharistic Prayer A also responds to the desire for greater vocal participation through the prayer by the congregation. In addition to the *Sanctus* and the memorial acclamations, it includes another acclamation, addressed to the Father: 'To you be glory and praise for ever', used six times and easily memorized, especially if sung, though it remains an optional addition. It ends with a congregational doxology from Revelation 5.13:

> **Blessing and honour and glory and power**
> **be yours for ever and ever.**
> **Amen.**

10

Eucharistic Prayer B

Although only part of Anglican liturgy since 1980, Eucharistic Prayer B has the deepest historical roots, being based on the Eucharistic Prayer in the third-century liturgy of St Hippolytus of Rome. Hippolytus himself speaks of his prayer as a received tradition, though that may refer more to shape and principle than text, and much of the actual wording may be the creative work of Hippolytus. The text, unused through most of Christian history, was revived through the work of Dom Bernard Botte, who incorporated many of its phrases into the current Roman Catholic Order of the Mass as its second Eucharistic Prayer. In the Church of England, in the preparation for *ASB*, Brian Brindley and Roger Beckwith worked with the text from Hippolytus and with the Roman prayer to produce an Anglican version. It is very little changed in *Common Worship*.

The Roman version conforms the shape of the prayer to the familiar 'Western' shape, with the invocation of the Spirit on the gifts before the institution narrative, and *Common Worship* stays with this. Some comparison of the Hippolytan text with *Common Worship* reveals some interesting theological strands. This preface in Hippolytus is where the most striking phrases are to be found.

> We render thanks to you, O God,
> through your beloved Son Jesus Christ,
> whom in the last times you have sent to us
> as a saviour and redeemer and angel of your will;
> who is your inseparable Word, through whom you have made
> all things;
> and in whom you were well pleased;
> whom you sent from heaven into a virgin's womb;

and who, being conceived in the womb,
was made flesh and was manifested as your Son,
being born of the Holy Spirit and the Virgin;
who, fulfilling your will and gaining for you a holy people,
stretched out his hands when he should suffer;
that he might release from suffering those who have believed
    in you.

In *Common Worship* this becomes

> Father, we give you thanks and praise
> through your beloved Son Jesus Christ, your living Word,
> through whom you have created all things;
> who was sent by you in your great goodness to be our Saviour.
>
> By the power of the Holy Spirit he took flesh;
> as your Son, born of the blessed Virgin,
> he lived on earth and went about among us;
> he opened wide his arms for us on the cross;
> he put an end to death by dying for us;
> and revealed the resurrection by rising to new life;
> so he fulfilled your will and won for you a holy people.

Although the language of Eucharistic Prayer B sounds very biblical, it is a collection of biblical allusions strung together in order to tell the key elements of who Jesus was. The prayer covers Jesus' relationship as beloved Son to God as Father (a relationship that enables us also to call God 'Father'), his pre-existence and presence at Creation, the fact that he was sent by God to save the world, the virgin birth and Incarnation, the love expressed in his death, his victory over death and inauguration of the new Creation and, finally, God's calling now of the Gentiles into covenantal relationship with himself. It is a remarkable piece of theology that, with very few words, weaves together the story of Jesus from the dawn of time to our life in Christ today.

One of the changes made in *Common Worship* relates to the phrase 'he lived on earth and went about among us', which is not directly part of the prayer of Hippolytus, nor of the Roman version. *ASB*, where this is the Third Eucharistic Prayer, has 'he was seen on earth and went about among us', but the *Common Worship* revisers thought this open to misinterpretation. 'Revealed the resurrection' is also an interesting phrase, which is drawn from a later point in Hippolytus, where these words introduce the institution narrative: 'When he was betrayed to voluntary suffering that he might destroy death, and break the bonds of the devil, and tread down hell, and shine upon the righteous, and fix a term, and manifest the resurrection, took bread . . .'

A further echo of Hippolytus lies in the clause 'we thank you for counting us worthy to stand in your presence and serve you', which draws on the words in Hippolytus: 'giving you thanks because you have held us worthy to stand before you and minister to you'.

Eucharistic Prayer B also draws on the Roman equivalent in two ways that are not foreshadowed in Hippolytus. In both cases they make elements of the Eucharistic Prayer more explicit in a way that subsequent prayers have followed. The first is in being very clear about the action of the Holy Spirit upon both the gifts and the people. It prays,

grant that by the power of your Holy Spirit,
and according to your holy will,
these gifts of bread and wine
may be to us the body and blood of our Lord Jesus Christ . . .

Send the Holy Spirit on your people
and gather into one in your kingdom
all who share this one bread and one cup . . .

Because this follows the Roman pattern, the invocations of the Spirit are separated by the institution narrative and the *anamnesis*, but subsequent prayers, whether they keep the two invocations separate or bring them together, have been equally clear that the action of the Holy Spirit is upon both the gifts and the elements.

The second emphasis, new in this prayer when it came into use in 1980, was the link with the life of heaven. Although all Eucharistic Prayers linked the praises of the community with the angels and the saints through the *Sanctus*, in words reminiscent of the Book of Common Prayer's 'therefore with Angels and Archangels, and with all the company of heaven', until the Third Eucharistic Prayer in *ASB* there had been no equivalent of 'we, in the company of all the saints, may praise and glorify you for ever'. Subsequent prayers have further enhanced that emphasis and, as in Prayer B, allowed for the naming of particular saints at this point in the prayer.

There are a number of other phrases that Brindley and Beckwith introduced in *ASB*. They were seeking to find ways of avoiding some of the theological language, especially in relation to offering and sacrifice, that had caused a stalemate and left both catholics and evangelicals dissatisfied with the texts that had been produced. Their *anamnesis* represented a fresh attempt, leaving behind the language of 'remember his offering of himself' and 'having in remembrance his death' and saying instead,

> calling to mind his death on the cross,
> his perfect sacrifice made once for the sins of all men,
> rejoicing at his mighty resurrection and glorious ascension
> and looking for his coming in glory,
> we celebrate this memorial of our redemption.

The bringing together of the verbs 'calling to mind', 'rejoicing', 'looking for' and 'celebrate' seemed to provide a way through. Their attempt apparently succeeded, for this prayer became widely used by people of every tradition and this paragraph went largely unrevised into *Common Worship*, save for the change from 'the sins of all men' to 'the sins of the whole world' in response to a greater sensitivity to gender-inclusive language.

11

Eucharistic Prayer C

Eucharistic Prayer C draws the Church of England back to the Reformation era and to Thomas Cranmer. Influenced by the continental reformers, the Second English Prayer Book of 1552 departed significantly from Catholic theology and liturgical practice, not least in the order of the prayers of the Eucharist. The flow of the Eucharistic Prayer was interrupted after the *Sanctus* by a devotional prayer ('the prayer of humble access', see Chapter 18) and after the words of institution by the reception of Communion, leaving the final part of the prayer, with its sense of self-offering and its doxology, until after the distribution. The central part of the prayer, with the narrative of the institution, but without any *epiclesis*, came to be called the 'prayer of consecration'. The 1662 wording, although it made some changes to the text and rubrics, did not challenge this arrangement, which became normative for the 300 years following.

But there were those, especially after the influences of the nineteenth-century Oxford Movement, with its desire to recover catholic theology and practice in the Church of England, who were unhappy with this rearrangement of the order and desired a return to the classic shape. This they achieved, without any change to the text, by joining the 'prayer of oblation', as the first prayer after Communion came to be called, to the prayer of consecration, adding the Lord's Prayer at that point and only then receiving the consecrated elements. This, though quite unofficial, became known as 'the Interim Rite' – it was always seen to be provisional. In a more radical rearrangement some also moved the prayer of humble access to a position before the dialogue and *Sanctus*, thus restoring the classic shape of the Eucharistic Prayer while using the 1662 text.

The Eucharistic Prayer of the Interim Rite is the forerunner of Eucharistic Prayer C. It was given its first formal approval in 'Series 1', where words were added to call to mind the death, resurrection and ascension of Jesus at the point where the prayer of consecration and the prayer of oblation are joined. It read:

> Do this in remembrance of me. Wherefore, O Lord and heavenly Father, we thy humble servants, having in remembrance the precious death and passion of thy dear Son, his mighty resurrection and glorious ascension, entirely desire thy fatherly goodness mercifully to accept this our sacrifice of praise and thanksgiving.

'Series 1' also provided a shorter version, in which the latter part of the prayer of oblation was kept for use after Communion. By the time of *ASB*, this prayer has been 'translated' into a more contemporary English style, has received some other more theologically motivated changes and has emerged as the Fourth Eucharistic Prayer of Rite A. With minimal further change, designed to bring the language back closer to 1662, it becomes Prayer C of *Common Worship* Order One. So what we have is a prayer that is a rather extraordinary compromise. It has a classic 'catholic' shape, a sixteenth-century text that is gently modernized but not simplified, a Reformation theology and an emphasis on the cross, but with the addition of an *epiclesis*, though one focused more obviously on the communicants than on the bread and wine.

> Hear us, merciful Father, we humbly pray,
> and grant that, by the power of your Holy Spirit,
> we receiving these gifts of your creation, this bread and this wine,
> according to your Son our Saviour Jesus Christ's holy institution,
> in remembrance of his death and passion,
> may be partakers of his most blessed body and blood . . .

Behind this passage lurks 1 Corinthians 10.16 and 11.23–25. The reference to Jesus Christ's holy institution of course brings to mind the institution narrative of 11.23–25, but the final phrase of this section, 'partakers of his most blessed body and blood', also draws our attention to the previous chapter (10.16). The word 'partake' is quite a good translation of the idea expressed by the Greek word *koinonia*, which is notoriously hard to put into English. *Koinonia* can mean something along the lines of 'participation', 'communion' or 'partnership'; the now somewhat archaic 'partake', as its form suggests, has the edge of a 'part share' and as such reminds us that receiving the body and blood requires more than just a remembrance of a historical event: it is the means – or at least one of them – by which we participate in the life of the dying and risen Christ.

The themes that dominate this prayer are the cross and the redemption won there, alongside a strong and repeated use of the language of oblation and sacrifice, though always with emphasis on the once-for-all nature of what happened on Good Friday.

> All glory be to you, our heavenly Father,
> who, in your tender mercy,
> gave your only Son our Saviour Jesus Christ
> to suffer death upon the cross for our redemption;
> who made there by his one oblation of himself once offered
> a full, perfect and sufficient sacrifice, oblation and satisfaction for
>   the sins of the whole world . . .

and later:

> Grant that by his merits and death,
> and through faith in his blood,
> we and all your Church may receive forgiveness of our sins
> and all other benefits of his passion.
> Although we are unworthy, through our manifold sins,
> to offer you any sacrifice,
> yet we pray that you will accept this
> the duty and service that we owe.
> Do not weigh our merits, but pardon our offences,
> and fill us all who share in this holy communion
> with your grace and heavenly blessing . . .

This prayer often quotes directly from the Bible and, as it does, weaves together certain evocative phrases that are drawn from various places throughout the Bible. So, for example, 'tender mercy' is drawn from Luke 1.78 from Zechariah's beautiful hymn of praise to God after John the Baptist's birth. There the tender mercy of God is what causes the dawn from on high to break upon us. The following phrase, 'gave your only Son', occurs in different forms throughout the New Testament, such as John 3.16 and Romans 8.32. Having said that, God giving his Son to suffer is never made explicit in the New Testament, though it is there implicitly in Romans 8.32.

This stringing together of a number of quotes from various places in the Bible is known by scholars as a 'catena' and has a long history within Christianity. There is even evidence that the New Testament authors themselves used this as a method of citing the Bible (see for example 1 Peter 2.6–8). This is a technique also beloved of liturgical writers, but it is particularly evident in this prayer.

Despite the wide variety of biblical quotations, Eucharistic Prayer C maintains a particular theological focus. If contemporary Eucharistic Prayers have a broad theological sweep from mention of Creation through to the gathering up of all things in Christ in the life of heaven, Eucharistic Prayer C keeps the focus on one world-changing event on a hill outside Jerusalem. If contemporary Eucharistic Prayers use words such a 'celebrate', 'meal', 'new creation' and 'friends', Eucharistic Prayer C is more interested in sacrifice and redemption. This is a prayer to a God who not so much looks with favour on his people as pardons their offences.

This prayer represents clearly and strongly a particular interpretation of the New Testament language of atonement that was especially popular at the time of the Reformation. Although the strands do not all occur in one place in the New Testament, the themes of sacrifice, of redemption, of sin and our need for forgiveness, and of Christ's once-only death that renders further sacrifice unnecessary, are all present at some point in the New Testament. It is in the book of Hebrews (7.27; 9.12; 10.2, 10) that the word translated 'once for all' – in Greek the word is *'ephapax* and means 'once affecting all time' – is used to differentiate Jesus' sacrifice from the sacrifices enacted by the priests in the Temple. In a number of places the author of Hebrews makes it clear that Jesus' offering of himself has now rendered all other future sacrifice redundant. Although the word is also used elsewhere in the New Testament (e.g. Romans 6.10; 1 Peter 3.18), it is not there linked with sacrifice. This emphasis illustrates quite how important debate was in the Reformation era about whether the 'Mass' could in fact be a sacrifice.

This prayer represents the desire to express absolute clarity about the fact that the Eucharist could not be a sacrifice since Jesus' death was the only sacrifice necessary. This compares with the Eucharistic Prayer of the Roman Mass, which spoke of 'the gifts we offer you in sacrifice' and asked God to 'accept', 'bless and approve our offering' and to

> Look with favour on these offerings and accept them as once you accepted the gifts of your servant Abel, the sacrifice of Abraham, our father in faith, and the bread and wine offered by your priest Melchisedech. Almighty God, we pray that your angel will take this sacrifice to your altar in heaven.

Also important is the way in which the prayer draws on Romans 3.24–25. These two verses are some of the most important yet most complex of Paul's writings. In them, he is attempting to put into words what he believes about the effect that Jesus' death had on people who have sinned (Romans 3.23). The challenge is that he uses a wide range of language and imagery in order to establish that those who have sinned are justified by grace. In the space of what is effectively one and a half verses Paul pulls together language of redemption ('through the redemption that is in Christ Jesus', 3.24), of sacrifice ('a sacrifice of atonement', 3.25) and of the Passover ('he had passed over the sins previously committed', 3.25).

Each one of these elements explains slightly differently what Jesus' death did. Redemption and Passover are straightforward metaphors. In redemption a slave or captive is bought back. At the Passover the angel of death passed over the firstborn sons of Israel, in the same way that God would 'pass over' the sins that had been committed. The sacrificial metaphor is much more complex, and we cannot even hope to do justice to it here.

Indeed the problem is the complexity of the theology of sacrifice. In Romans 3.24–25, alongside his metaphors of redemption and Passover, Paul is pulling on the metaphor of the sacrificial system. The key question that remains unclear is what *he* thought happened as a result of the sacrifices in the Temple. The Temple sacrifices dealt with the inadvertent sins of faithful Israelites. The question is: what did such sacrifices do? Some believe that they 'propitiated' or pleased God; as a result he was no longer angered by the sin. Others believe that they actually wiped out the sin (a process known as 'expiation'), so that it no longer existed. Others still would argue that neither propitiation nor expiation quite do justice to the Old Testament understanding of sacrifice and sin.

As a result, it is hard to know precisely what Paul meant in Romans 3.24–25. This is made an even greater challenge by the fact that there is little agreement even about what word to use to translate the Greek word *hilasterion*, since the word means both the place where atonement took place (i.e. the mercy seat) and the means by which it happened (propitiation or expiation). All we can tell is that Paul is making a significant statement about Jesus and sacrifice: God put him forward to be the place *and* the means by which sins are forgiven.

It is also worth noticing that there is now a shift in understanding even of how to translate the verse. Prayer C talks about 'faith in his blood', which is a direct reference to the King James

Version translation, 'whom God hath set forth *to be* a propitiation through faith in his blood'. Many, though not all, scholars
would now argue that it is better to rearrange the words, so

- the NRSV has 'a sacrifice of atonement by his blood, effective
  through faith';
- the ESV has 'whom God put forward as a propitiation by his
  blood to be received by faith';
- the NIV has 'God presented Christ as a sacrifice of atonement,
  through the shedding of his blood – to be received by faith'.

As we can see, the word order has shifted from having faith
in the blood to the blood being part of the sacrifice, and faith
becoming the more general concept of believing, not just in
blood but in Jesus himself. This shift in usage makes the phrase
'faith in his blood' stand out in this prayer as reflecting a translation that many would no longer support.

Despite the importance of the doctrine of atonement in this
prayer, Eucharistic Prayer C has made the decision to follow
Paul in not deciding definitively how the atonement of Jesus
was effective. Although to many modern eyes the prayer, and
the sentiments behind it, are monochrome arguments about
the forgiveness of sins, in fact both Romans 3.24–25, which
lies behind this prayer, and the prayer itself use a number of
images to explore the idea. As we saw above, Paul uses redemption, sacrifice and the Passover as images of the forgiveness of
sin. Intriguingly, of these, Prayer C has dropped Passover but
kept redemption.

Additional variety has been included in the prayer by adding
the words 'oblation' and 'satisfaction' in the phrase 'a full, perfect
and sufficient sacrifice, oblation and satisfaction'. The word
'oblation', though very close in meaning to 'sacrifice', comes
from the Latin word for 'offer' and so has more of the nuance
of 'offering'. As a result it draws on Hebrew 10.5ff., where the
coupling of sacrifice and offering is repeated seven times. The
inclusion of the word 'satisfaction' also allows the introduction

of the satisfaction atonement theory (a theory particularly associated with St Anselm of Canterbury but not explicit in much of the New Testament).

As a result, Prayer C is much less monochrome than it might at first appear. It is, of course, focused closely on atonement but it does not prejudge or close down the different models or images of atonement that one might adopt. Its carefully chosen wording weaves together redemption, sacrifice, offering and satisfaction, all as images of what Jesus' death achieved. It arises clearly out of its original context in which concern about the efficacy of the atonement, and the connection of the Eucharist to this, was one of the hot topics of the day.

12

Eucharistic Prayer D

Eucharistic Prayer D is something different, in every way far removed from Prayer C. It was specially written for *Common Worship*, drafted by Bishop James Jones of Liverpool in consultation with his children, though worked on and developed within the Liturgical Commission. With its strong narrative style, its vibrant concrete images, its easy rhythms, its responsive acclamations and its comparative brevity, it was intended to appeal to congregations that included families and children.

We have already explored its version of the words of institution (see Chapter 8). It is worth exploring the rest of the text in full, returning at the end to the acclamations.

> Almighty God, good Father to us all,
> your face is turned towards your world.
> In love you gave us Jesus your Son
> to rescue us from sin and death.
> Your Word goes out to call us home to the city where angels sing
>   your praise.
> We join with them in heaven's song . . .
>
> Father of all, we give you thanks for every gift that comes from
>   heaven.
>
> To the darkness Jesus came as your light.
> With signs of faith and words of hope
> he touched untouchables with love and washed the guilty clean . . .
>
> The crowds came out to see your Son, yet at the end they
>   turned on him.
> On the night he was betrayed
> he came to table with his friends to celebrate the freedom of
>   your people.

... Therefore, Father, with this bread and this cup
we celebrate the cross
on which he died to set us free.
Defying death he rose again
and is alive with you to plead for us and all the world ...

Send your Spirit on us now
that by these gifts we may feed on Christ with opened eyes
    and hearts on fire.

May we and all who share this food
offer ourselves to live for you
and be welcomed at your feast in heaven where all creation
    worships you,
Father, Son and Holy Spirit ...

Prayer D is one of those that has adopted a single *epiclesis* over the gifts and the people at the later point in the prayer after the narrative of institution. Some have regarded the wording 'Send your Spirit on us now that by these gifts we may feed on Christ' as being less than adequate, since it is unclear whether the Spirit is sent on the gifts.

The text is punctuated by a repeated acclamation. 'This is *his* story,' says or sings the president or the deacon and, later, 'This is *our* story' (emphasis added in each case). The narrative style of the prayer is underlined by affirming that the story of Jesus engages with the story of our lives and ours with his. The response is to turn narrative into praise – 'This is our song' – and, in an extension of the *Sanctus*, 'Hosanna in the highest.'

This prayer does not so much quote Scripture as exude it. This is a prayer that has absorbed many passages and phrases and much theology, and has placed it together in a poetic summary of salvation. Although Prayer D shares with Prayer C a drawing from a wide variety of biblical texts, there the similarities end. In C, the moment of salvation is seen very clearly as being Jesus' death; here the whole of Jesus' life, death, resurrection and ascension are included. In Prayer C the major metaphor of atonement was sacrifice in its various forms; here the major metaphor is a combination of the whole exodus story with that of the prodigal son. Prayer C is clear about its theology and states it firmly; here the theology is more allusive and thought-provoking.

The prayer opens with the use of a favourite Old Testament image of God turning his face towards his people. The image of God's face being turned both away from and towards his people runs throughout the Old Testament. So for example Psalm 27.9 begs God not to turn his face away; in a similar way 2 Chronicles 30.9 assures those returning from exile that God will not turn his face away from them. The image is extended throughout the Old Testament to be a poetic description of the state of relationship that existed between God and his people. When they turned away, God also turned away. When they turned back (i.e. repented) God was urged, often in the Psalms, also to turn back and face his people. This prayer begins, then, with the assurance that God's default position is to stand with his face turned towards us, his people, ready to receive us when we turn towards him.

The language of atonement it uses comes from the same Pauline passage as that of Eucharistic Prayer C but focuses on a different image. We noted in the previous chapter that Paul uses 'Passover' in Romans 3.24–25 as one of his images of atonement. This prayer, as many people have done throughout Christian history, extends the image of Passover (i.e. the angel of the Lord passing over the firstborn son) to include the exodus as a whole, so the theme of rescuing from slavery and freedom is woven throughout the prayer. As a result, Jesus' death is seen to free us from slavery to sin just as Moses freed God's people from slavery to the Egyptians.

Another interesting example of rich allusive theology is the line 'Your Word goes out to call us home'. In this simple phrase is the suggestion of God's 'Word' (which can equally be understood to mean God's creative word from Genesis 1, which called the world into being, and Jesus the Word from John 1), which is what summons us to go home to a Father who loves us. Although this is not an explicit reference to the prodigal son, it is hard to evoke language of a loving father – as this prayer does – and the concept of being called home without making us think of the prodigal son's welcome home by his loving father. The next line makes it clear that our home in this instance is to be found at the end of all times and is the city, the new Jerusalem, of Revelation 21.2.

From here the prayer moves on to Jesus' life and ministry, drawing together the language of light shining in the darkness – which can be found both in Old Testament prophecy such as Isaiah 9.2 and in John's Gospel (1.5) – with Jesus' love and touch of those on the outskirts of society in the healing miracles. As a result, Jesus' life and ministry become an important focus of this narrative of salvation.

As mentioned above, this prayer is allusive and poetic; it does not so much state theology as evoke it. Its language suggests a spaciousness within which the members of the congregation are to think their own thoughts about the impact of Jesus' life, death, resurrection and ascension. The challenge of this is that it requires a certain level of theological and biblical literacy in order to understand the depth and breadth of the many references being alluded to in the prayer, though at the same time we don't have to be aware of the allusions and their significance to appreciate the poetic language being used.

13

Eucharistic Prayer E

Eucharistic Prayer E is another new prayer created for *Common Worship*, initially the work of Canon Jeremy Haselock. The intention was to produce a classic 'Western' Eucharistic Prayer, in the sense of one that has the *epiclesis* before the narrative of the institution, that has all that such a prayer ought to have, but with a lighter touch in terms of the complexity of language. So there is both brevity and simplicity, yet nothing is missing.

One feature that illustrates this intention is the preface.

> Father, you made the world and love your creation.
> You gave your Son Jesus Christ to be our Saviour.
> His dying and rising have set us free from sin and death.
> And so we gladly thank you,
> with saints and angels praising you . . .

For all its brevity, this celebrates the mighty acts of God in Creation and in the life, death and resurrection of Jesus, and joins us to the worship of heaven. It is also a 'default' preface since another feature of this prayer is the replacement of this preface by one of the extended prefaces discussed in Chapter 7.

The *epiclesis* differs from other prayers in that, although it adopts the Western position, at that point it brings together prayer for the Spirit to come upon both the bread and wine and the people, so that the two are held together.

> We praise and bless you, loving Father,
> through Jesus Christ, our Lord;
> and as we obey his command,
> send your Holy Spirit,
> that broken bread and wine outpoured
> may be for us the body and blood of your dear Son.

This is also one of two prayers (the other is Eucharistic Prayer G) that uses the phrase 'we plead with confidence' as it finds new language to express the work of Jesus in the *anamnesis*.

> So, Father, we remember all that Jesus did,
> in him we plead with confidence his sacrifice made once for all
>   upon the cross.
>
> Bringing before you the bread of life and cup of salvation,
> we proclaim his death and resurrection
> until he comes in glory.

In some ways this prayer overlaps with Eucharistic Prayer C in that it picks up the 'once for all' sacrificial imagery of atonement that was so important for that prayer. What is different is the phrase 'plead with confidence'. This phrase has had a mixed reception. Some believe that it is not possible to plead with confidence since pleading implies a lack of confidence. The problem here is the word 'plead', which in modern parlance suggests an emotional appeal. The usage here is closer to legal language, which is more along the lines of putting forward an argument. This is something we can do with confidence, a confidence that the apostle Paul would certainly support since it has the sense of having 'confidence' in Christ (see for example 2 Corinthians 3.4; 5.8; Ephesians 3.12; and so on). It is 'in him' that we can plead with this level of confidence, since in Christ our identity is transformed through his death and resurrection.

The second half of this section turns attention to the bread of life and cup of salvation. The phrase 'the bread of life' is obviously from John's Gospel (e.g. 6.35), but the 'cup of salvation' is of Old Testament origin and can be found in places like Psalm 116.13. It is unclear precisely what this cup of salvation was, but it was probably a part of the sacrificial cult in the Temple that might have been poured out during a sacrifice. As a phrase it describes perfectly the significance of the cup from which we drink in the Eucharist.

From here the prayer returns to the language of 1 Corinthians 11.26, which talks about eating the bread and drinking the cup as the proclamation of Jesus' death until he comes. This is a phrase that, for obvious reasons, is used on a regular basis in a number of Eucharistic Prayers. It is probably worth observing that this phrasing is interesting since it is an action – albeit an action accompanied with words – that functions as proclamation here. It is easy to assume that proclamation must always entail speaking. This most important of proclamations about Christ's death is enacted more than it is spoken.

Prayer E also has a strong forward thrust in terms of the kingdom of God in both earth and heaven.

> Lord of all life,
> help us to work together for that day
> when your kingdom comes
> and justice and mercy will be seen in all the earth.
>
> Look with favour on your people,
> gather us in your loving arms
> and bring us with [*N and*] all the saints
> to feast at your table in heaven.

One of the challenges of the decision to use brief language is that sometimes it needs unpacking in order to make sense. A good example of this occurs in this prayer, where the words 'Lord of all life, help us to work together for that day when your kingdom comes' seem to imply that the full coming of God's kingdom relies on our own efforts, and that only when we have worked together well enough for justice and mercy will God's kingdom come.

This clearly cannot be the case. Instead the theology that lies behind this phrase involves the idea that as Christians we seek to live the new Creation – which is marked by justice and mercy – in the present. Although it is not and cannot be fully present, our vocation is to work alongside one another as though we already lived in a world in which God's kingdom had come.

The coupling here of the coming of God's kingdom with justice and mercy is a bringing together of an explicit New Testament phrase with explicit Old Testament language. While Jesus is clearly passionate about justice and mercy, this phrase is never used as a description of God's kingdom in the Gospels. 'Justice and mercy' is language that is found more often in the Old Testament, such as in Hosea 2.19, though there 'steadfast love' (or 'loving kindness') is also used alongside the other two terms.

Living and working together with justice, mercy and steadfast love means that, when the day does come, we will be ready with our oil lamps filled and our eyes wide open like the bridesmaids in Matthew 25 waiting for the bridegroom to come. At that point we will not only sit down to eat at the wedding banquet; we will also be gathered into the loving arms of God, an image that suggests not only the yearning of Jesus to gather Jerusalem like a hen gathers her brood but also God, in Hosea 11.3, who taught toddler Israel to walk and scooped them into his arms when they looked like they might fall. The tender parenting image alongside the wedding banquet here joins profound love and protection with celebration.

14

Eucharistic Prayer F

Prayer F is probably the richest prayer in terms of its theology and strong memorable images. Its origins lie in the fourth-century Eucharistic Prayer of St Basil, still in occasional use in the Eastern churches. In the West it has been experienced, in a very modified form, as Eucharistic Prayer 4 of the Roman rite – but there remodelled to fit the traditional Western shape – and as Eucharistic Prayer D of the 1977 Book of Common Prayer of the Episcopal Church of the USA, both of which stay closer to the original text than does Prayer F of *Common Worship*.

In terms of the text, the interest lies particularly in the preface and indeed in all the words before the institution narrative.

> You are worthy of our thanks and praise,
> Lord God of truth,
> for by the breath of your mouth
> you have spoken your word,
> and all things have come into being.
>
> You fashioned us in your image
> and placed us in the garden of your delight.
> Though we chose the path of rebellion
> you would not abandon your own.

The text draws on the image of the 'garden of [God's] delight', which is lost in the Roman and American versions, preferring a picture of humankind enjoying the Creation to theirs, where the emphasis is on humankind having dominion over the Creation.

The Roman text at this point reads:

> you have fashioned all your works in wisdom and in love. You formed man in your own image and entrusted the whole world

to his care, so that, in serving you alone, the Creator, he might have dominion over all creatures. And when through disobedience he had lost your friendship, you did not abandon him to the domain of death.

For many people the idea of humanity having dominion over all creatures is a difficult one since a certain interpretation of this can be seen to have led to an abusive relationship between humanity and the environment. One of the interesting questions people raise is the best translation of Genesis 1.26: 'let them have dominion over . . .' The Hebrew word *radah* can mean 'to have dominion' but more often means 'to rule'. In the context of the rest of the verse (in which humanity is created in the image of God), this seems to suggest that there is a connection between being created in the image of God and 'ruling' over Creation. In other words humanity is created to be to Creation what God is: ruling over the world only as the Creator would do.

Nevertheless, the image of being placed in the garden of delight is much easier to relate to without additional explanation, and communicates evocatively the wonder of existence in the Garden of Eden. *Common Worship* also omits the idea of disobedience leading to the loss of friendship between God and his people. It continues:

Again and again you drew us into your covenant of grace.
You gave your people the law and taught us by your prophets
to look for your reign of justice, mercy and peace.

Again the text is interesting for abandoning the word 'salvation' in favour of 'your reign of justice, mercy and peace'. The effect of this is to focus the narrative much more clearly on the Old Testament and on the prophets, where the words 'justice', 'mercy', 'peace', 'righteousness' and 'loving kindness' often feature together as the principles of God's reign. Rome has 'Time and time again you offered them covenants and through the prophets taught them to look forward to salvation.'

After the *Sanctus* the prayer continues:

> Lord God, you are the most holy one,
> enthroned in splendour and light,
> yet in the coming of your Son Jesus Christ
> you reveal the power of your love
> made perfect in our human weakness.

The Eastern original and the Roman and American versions all make more of the sense of God enthroned in splendour and light at the beginning of the prayer. The Roman prayer reads:

> You are the one God living and true, existing before all ages and abiding for all eternity, dwelling in unapproachable light; yet you, who alone are good, the source of life, have made all that is, so that you might fill your creatures with blessings and bring joy to many of them by the glory of your light.

In Prayer F this is reduced, at a later point in the text, to 'you are the most holy one, enthroned in splendour and light'. It continues:

> Embracing our humanity,
> Jesus showed us the way of salvation;
> loving us to the end,
> he gave himself to death for us;
> dying for his own,
> he set us free from the bonds of sin,
> that we might rise and reign with him in glory.
>
> On the night he gave up himself for us all
> he took bread and gave you thanks . . .

One of the key emphases of this prayer is that salvation is to be found in the whole of Jesus' life, death and resurrection. It was his embracing of humanity – with all the resonances of Philippians 2.5–11 that this implies – that showed us the way to salvation, his death that freed us from the bonds of sin and his resurrection that gave us a new way of being that allows us to reign with him in glory.

The phrase 'he gave up himself', which reflects both the Liturgy of St Basil and the Roman rite, is a striking variant on 'in which he was betrayed'. This emphasis reflects a leaning towards Johannine theology. Where the Synoptic Gospels highlight the betrayal of Jesus, John implies that Jesus was greatly in control of events and only died when he 'gave up his spirit' (John 19.30). Prayers E and G have 'the night before he died', and as a result are much closer to the Synoptic tradition on Jesus' death.

Prayer F then continues with the most common form of the institution narrative.

The *anamnesis* and *epiclesis* are not much different from those in the other prayers. Most of the verbs in the *anamnesis* are common to the other prayers, but the 'longing' for Christ's coming is stronger than the more usual 'looking for', and the description of the resurrection as 'his bursting from the tomb' is a striking image and, as with the language about Jesus' death, stresses quite strongly that Jesus was in control of all the events from his death to resurrection. The *epiclesis* is a single invocation on the gifts and the people. It includes a prayer, not found elsewhere, that God will 'make us a perfect offering in [his] sight.'

> Therefore we proclaim the death that he suffered on the cross,
> we celebrate his resurrection, his bursting from the tomb,
> we rejoice that he reigns at your right hand on high
> and we long for his coming in glory.
>
> As we recall the one, perfect sacrifice of our redemption,
> Father, by your Holy Spirit let these gifts of your creation
> be to us the body and blood of our Lord Jesus Christ;
> form us into the likeness of Christ
> and make us a perfect offering in your sight.

There follows one of the novel features of this and Prayer G: the inclusion of a brief paragraph of intercession, absent from Church of England liturgy since 1552 (see Chapter 5).

> Look with favour on your people
> and in your mercy hear the cry of our hearts.
> Bless the earth,
> heal the sick,
> let the oppressed go free
> and fill your Church with power from on high.

The plea that God should hear the cry of our hearts is a vital strand throughout the Bible, beginning in Exodus 3.7 and continuing onwards; although God appears to be portrayed as being far away, this strand reminds us time and time again that he is in fact very close indeed, straining to hear us when we cry out to him. The four invocations following this, however, are slightly unusual. The most common connections between blessing and the earth in the Bible are either a blessing of the *people* of the earth (e.g. Genesis 26.4; Psalm 134.3) or a call on the earth to bless God (Psalm 67.5). What is unclear here is whether 'the earth' means the created cosmos or those who live in it. If the latter, then the first invocation is the general summary of which the following three invocations (heal the sick etc.) are an explanation (i.e. bless the earth *by* healing the sick etc.). If the former is what is in mind, then this is a plea to God to bless the world he created, presumably by making it fertile.

Of the three invocations following 'Bless the earth', the plea to heal the sick and free the oppressed seems drawn from Isaiah 61.1 via Jesus' use of it in his synagogue sermon in Luke 4.18, and the request for power from on high picks up the reference to the sending of the Spirit on the disciples that Jesus promised in Luke 24.49.

Like other prayers, Prayer F moves towards the doxology with a reference to the saints and to God's 'table' in heaven and a return to the Creation theme. In Prayer F, uniquely, it speaks of bringing the new Creation 'to perfection'. This draws on a strong strand of theology that is found particularly in Paul. Passages like 2 Corinthians 5.17 declare that the new Creation is present whenever anyone is in Christ, while at the same time in Romans 8.21–22 the apostle talks of the Creation groaning while it waits for freedom from bondage. Taken together these imply that the new Creation has indeed broken in on the world, but we nevertheless still wait for the moment when it will be perfected at the end of all times. These words direct our attention forwards to that time, also using language, from Mark 13.27, about the angels gathering the elect from the ends of earth (though omitting the reference to the ends of heaven that is also in Mark 13).

> Gather your people from the ends of the earth
> to feast with [*N and*] and all your saints
> at the table in your kingdom,
> where the new creation is brought to perfection
> in Jesus Christ our Lord.

The prayer includes, optionally, a number of acclamations, reminiscent of Eastern liturgy, but not lifted directly from the Eucharistic Prayer of St Basil. Moving through the prayer, they begin with 'Amen. Lord, we believe', at the time of the *anamnesis* become 'Amen. Come, Lord Jesus' and, after the *epiclesis*, take the form 'Amen. Come, Holy Spirit.' At their best they are sung texts, repeated by the congregation after a deacon or cantor, and they punctuate what is otherwise a very long and rich presidential text.

15

Eucharistic Prayer G

Eucharistic Prayer G has had a difficult history. It was first created within the Roman Catholic International Commission for English in the Liturgy and published in 1984. It received attention from Bishop Kenneth Stevenson, who worked on it to produce one of the four Eucharistic Prayers included in *Patterns for Worship*, a report by the Liturgical Commission in 1989. There were significant departures from the Roman original, not least in bringing the two invocations of the Spirit together and rephrasing the language of offering and sacrifice. 'But,' the Introduction to *Patterns for Worship* explained, 'the vivid use of paradox which is one of the features of the original has been retained and is the explanation for such phrases as "silent music" and "these gifts which we bring before you from your own creation".' In addition the prayer included a series of 'triplets' – three two-line insertions for seasons and themes to draw out the particular emphasis of that day's celebration.

However, just as the Roman Catholic original text lay unused, so also the Anglican variant failed to receive approval. The General Synod rejected all four prayers, together with two other drafts, in 1996. This prayer might have disappeared entirely from liturgical sight had Richard Harries, then Bishop of Oxford, not persuaded the Revision Committee on the *Common Worship* Eucharistic Prayers to bring back a version of it, not greatly changed, except for the replacement of the 'triplets' by three standard invariable sentences and the introduction of intercession material.

The invariable preface, unchanged from the 1989 version, reads:

Blessed are you, Lord God,
our light and our salvation;
to you be glory and praise for ever.

From the beginning you have created all things
and all your works echo the silent music of your praise.
In the fullness of time you made us in your image,
the crown of all creation.

You give us breath and speech, that with angels and archangels
and all the powers of heaven
we may find a voice to sing your praise . . .

The opening words of this prayer immediately give it a more Jewish tone. The formula 'Blessed are you . . .' is an ancient Jewish way of opening prayer. It can be found in places like 1 Chronicles 29.10, is picked up in various New Testament texts like 2 Corinthians 1.3 and became widely used later in Judaism as a formula for prayer. This particular formulation beginning 'Blessed are you . . .' and ending 'glory and praise for ever' is taken from the apocryphal text the Prayer of Azariah 1.29ff., which repeats the words of the blessing and the link between glory and praise over and over again.

One of the main objections to this prayer was that some of the more poetic turns of phrase, such as 'silent music', if taken too literally appear to make little sense. In fact the above phrase is drawn from a passage by St John of the Cross in which he expresses his love of Creation, a use that is echoed directly here.

After the *Sanctus* the prayer continues:

How wonderful the work of your hands, O Lord.
As a mother tenderly gathers her children,
you embraced a people as your own.
When they turned away and rebelled
your love remained steadfast.

From them you raised up Jesus our Saviour, born of Mary,
to be the living bread,
in whom all our hungers are satisfied.

> He offered his life for sinners,
> and with a love stronger than death
> he opened wide his arms on the cross.

This section opens with a line that could be a paraphrase of psalms like Psalm 8 or 19, but in this exact formulation is used as the opening line of a popular 'traditional' but anonymous Jewish prayer. It moves from there to a strikingly feminine image, which combines Isaiah 66.13 – 'As a mother comforts her child, so I will comfort you' – with Jesus' evocative wish to gather Jerusalem under his wings as a mother hen does her brood (Matthew 23.37). The gathering element comes from Matthew and the explicit reference to God as a mother from Isaiah.

The remaining words of this section allude to the many references to Israel's rebellion throughout the Psalms and the prophets (see for example Psalm 78), to Jesus as the living bread in John 6.51, and even to love being stronger than death from the Song of Solomon 8.6. The effect of this is to juxtapose four strong and striking images (a mother with her child, servants rebelling against their master, a hungry people fed by bread, and love withstanding all assaults including floods (see Song of Solomon 8.7).

The words of institution follow the usual conventions. The *anamnesis* is one of only two prayers (with Prayer D) that celebrate the intercession of Christ with the Father.

> Father, we plead with confidence
> his sacrifice made once for all upon the cross;
> we remember his dying and rising in glory,
> and we rejoice that he intercedes for us at your right hand.

The *epiclesis*, which reads:

> Pour out your Holy Spirit as we bring before you
> these gifts of your creation;
> may they be for us the body and blood of your dear Son

is an interesting rewrite of the 1989 text:

> Pour out your Holy Spirit over us and these gifts
> which we bring before you from your own creation;
> Show them to be for us the body and blood of your dear Son.

Despite the strong resonance with Joel 2.28 and hence Acts 2.17, there was much debate about whether 'pouring out' was an appropriate way to speak of how the Holy Spirit came, but the term has survived. But 'showing them to be' has disappeared as a way of speaking of what happens in the Eucharistic Prayer. Prayer G adds to the *epiclesis* words based on the redundant Eucharistic Prayer 2 from *ASB*.

> As we eat and drink these holy things in your presence,
> form us in the likeness of Christ,
> and build us into a living temple to your glory.

Optional intercession follows. Unlike Prayer F, where the short text is invariable, Prayer G permits, perhaps invites, variable and spontaneous interpolation at the discretion of the president, while at the same time encouraging a much more explicit church focus, unlike Prayer F, which calls to mind Creation, the sick and the oppressed as well as the Church.

> [Remember, Lord, your Church in every land.
> Reveal her unity, guard her faith,
> and preserve her in peace . . .]

This is a slightly tame and less adventurous version of one of the 'triplets' in the 1989 text: 'Remember your Church in every land, redeemed by the blood of your Christ. Reveal her unity, guard her faith, and preserve her in peace. Remember all who minister in your Church . . . Remember those baptized this day . . .'

The prayer then moves, through mention of the saints, to the doxology and to the same acclamation (Revelation 5.13) with which Prayer A concludes.

16

Eucharistic Prayer H

Eucharistic Prayer H, when authorized in *Common Worship*, had no precedent in English Anglican provision. One would search in vain in every rite between 1549 and 1980 for anything like it. Its two most significant features are the part it assigns to the whole congregation and the position of the *Sanctus*.

It was introduced at the very last minute into the *Common Worship* provision. The Liturgical Commission had proposed six Eucharistic Prayers, but out of the revision process emerged eight. The pressure was for another prayer that went beyond Prayers A, D and F in terms of congregational vocal participation. All three of those prayers have congregational acclamations built in, but they are essentially responses, mainly unchanging, and the prayer is liturgically complete even when they are omitted. Not so with Prayer H, where the omission of the congregational words would render the prayer entirely unsatisfactory, not least in the omission of any reference to the cross. The logic and development of the prayer lies as much in the congregational words as in the president's part. To achieve this and to retain brevity, the prayer is economical in its language in a way that deprives it of some beauty and subtlety. If it were the only Eucharistic Prayer it would be an impoverishment and, when it is the only Eucharistic Prayer used in a particular community, it is that; but as part of a larger collection, it has its proper place.

Because of the congregational part, the whole prayer – other than the dialogue – is reproduced here.

> It is right to praise you, Father, Lord of all creation;
> in your love you made us for yourself.

When we turned away
you did not reject us,
but came to meet us in your Son.
**You embraced us as your children
and welcomed us to sit and eat with you.**

In Christ you shared our life
that we might live in him and he in us.
**He opened his arms of love upon the cross
and made for all the perfect sacrifice for sin.**

On the night he was betrayed,
at supper with his friends
he took bread, and gave you thanks;
he broke it and gave it to them, saying:
Take, eat; this is my body which is given for you;
do this in remembrance of me.
**Father, we do this remembrance of him:
his body is the bread of life.**

At the end of supper; taking the cup of wine,
he gave you thanks, and said:
Drink this, all of you; this is my blood of the new covenant,
which is shed for you for the forgiveness of sins;
do this in remembrance of me.
**Father, we do this in remembrance of him:
his blood is shed for all.**

As we proclaim his death and celebrate his rising in glory,
send your Holy Spirit that this bread and this wine
may be to us the body and blood of your dear Son.

**As we eat and drink these holy gifts
make us one in Christ, our risen Lord.**

With your whole Church throughout the world
we offer you this sacrifice of praise
and lift our voice to join the eternal song of heaven:

**Holy, holy, holy Lord,
God of power and might,**

Heaven and earth are full of your glory.
Hosanna in the highest.

One of the important features of this prayer is the recognition
that its opening lines are based profoundly on Luke 15.11–32:
the turning away, the coming to meet us, the sitting down to eat
at a feast and the arms open to embrace all evoke a paraphrase of
the well-loved story of the prodigal son which, though popular
elsewhere, here becomes the controlling metaphor for the story
of salvation. The following four lines summarize Christ's Incarnation and sacrificial death, before turning directly to the words
of institution.

The other unusual feature of the prayer is that it ends with
the *Sanctus*. To end with the *Sanctus* is novel in Anglican liturgy.
There is some evidence that it was acceptable in the early
centuries and some instances of it occur at the Reformation.
It ensures that the prayer ends caught up in the life of heaven,
but the omission of a doxology and even more so of the 'Amen'
will continue to leave some feeling this is a less than satisfactory prayer.

17

Breaking the bread

The breaking of the bread is the third of the four actions of Jesus at the last supper: taking, giving thanks, breaking, giving. At a certain level it is a purely utilitarian action: bread needs to be broken if it is to be shared. But the 'fraction', as it is often called, is also significant theologically, both in asserting something about the unity and diversity of the Church, the body of Christ, but also about its brokenness, which reflects the truth that it was the broken body of the crucified Christ that redeems.

The starting point is 1549, where Cranmer includes two texts, the first immediately after the Peace.

> Christ our paschal lamb is offered up for us, once for all, when he bare our sins in his body upon the cross, for he is the very lamb of God, that taketh away the sins of the world: wherefore let us keep a joyful and holy feast with the Lord.

A little later, during the distribution, the clerks are to sing *Agnus Dei*:

> ii O lamb of God, that takest away the sins of the world: have mercy upon us. O lamb of God, that takest away the sins of the world: grant us thy peace.

And in a fascinating rubric printed at the end of the rite, Cranmer says that the bread should be round, unleavened, as it was before, but something larger and thicker than had been the custom, so that it may be divided into pieces 'and every one shall be divided in two pieces at the very least'. He recognized that it was important that it should be broken bread that each received.

The 1552 text omitted both texts and gave new directions about the bread: 'It shall suffice that the bread be such as is usual to be eaten at the table with other meats, but the best and purest wheat bread.' Nothing is said about breaking it, though clearly breaking it would be necessary. The 1662 order directs the priest to break the bread during the prayer of consecration; 1928 makes no change. 'Series 1' directs that the bread shall be broken either during the prayer of consecration or at the Peace immediately before the distribution, with the option of using also *Agnus Dei*, with the same text as in 1549. 'Series 2' removes the option of breaking the bread during the Eucharistic Prayer and makes it a mandatory action – 'Then shall the consecrated bread be broken into pieces' – with two optional texts. The first was 1 Corinthians 10.16–17.

> The cup of blessing which we bless,
> is it not a sharing of the Blood of Christ?
> The bread which we break,
> is it not a sharing of the Body of Christ?
> We being many are one bread, one Body,
> for we all partake of the one bread.

The second was *Agnus Dei* as before. This is an anthem traced back to at least the fifth century, where it has a place in the Liturgy of St James. It draws on John 1.29 and Revelation 5.6, 12–13, and is probably of Syrian origin. It was designed to cover the bread-breaking, which could take some time, and started life as a simple chant to be repeated over and over again until the task was complete. Only later did liturgists tidy it up and make it inflexible, restricted to three clauses. At that point the musicians took over, creating elaborate settings that made it unsuitable at that point in the liturgy, which is what led some churches to relocate it during the distribution.

'Series 3' made three changes to the provision for the breaking of the bread. First it simplified the quotation from 1 Corinthians, removed the reference to the cup and turned a rhetorical question into a statement.

We break this bread
to share in the body of Christ.
**Though we are many, we are one body,
because we all share in one bread.**

Although the 'Series 3' words are clearer than Cranmer's originals, the question of the complexity of Paul's use of language about the body of Christ in 1 Corinthians nevertheless remains. Cranmer's use of the longer quote from 1 Corinthians 10.16–17 draws attention to the fluidity in Paul's language about the body of Christ in 1 Corinthians 10—11. In particular the question that emerges is what the phrases 'blood of Christ' and 'body of Christ' refer to in 10.16. The use of the blood of Christ at first suggests that Paul is only talking about the way in which the elements allow us a 'sharing' of the blood/body of Christ, but by verse 17 the movement from the bread to us indicates that something much more subtle is going on in his theology.

The key lies in the word translated 'sharing'. This translates the Greek word *koinonia* and has the suggestion of partnership or participation about it: participation in Christ and by extension also with each other. The bread/wine is the symbol that both draws us into that dynamic of participation and expresses the participation with one another that then occurs. The breaking of the bread, then, symbolizes our individual participation in something that catches us up into a corporate experience. The modern wording reminds us every time that breaking and sharing the bread is a symbol of our participation in Christ's body.

A second change in 'Series 3' was to provide a new version of the *Agnus Dei*. It was more a paraphrase than a translation. Believing that people had difficulty in unpacking the meaning of the phrase 'Lamb of God', Geoffrey Cuming created this text:

**Jesus, Lamb of God: have mercy on us.
Jesus, bearer of our sins: have mercy on us.
Jesus, redeemer of the world: give us your peace.**

The effect of this unpacking is to introduce some additional very specific ideas into the *Agnus Dei*. The second line draws the servant song in Isaiah (particularly 53.12 where the servant is said to have borne the sins of many) into the Johannine language of the Lamb of God taking away sin. The additional insertion of the idea of Jesus as the redeemer of the world ties the atonement achieved by the Lamb, who bore our sins, to the buying back of people enslaved to sin (rather than another image of atonement). Where John 1.29 leaves open the question of how the Lamb of God took away the sin of the world, this reinterpretation focuses it in one particular direction. In fact the Johannine language of the 'Lamb of God' suggests a Passover image for the atonement and it is, perhaps, a pity that this was not the image chosen to help unpack the sparse language of the *Agnus Dei* further.

The third change in 'Series 3' was that, in a rather backward liturgical move, it removed this text from the breaking of the bread and relegated it to the period of the distribution.

ASB left the modified 1 Corinthians text in place and printed two versions of the *Agnus Dei*, the one found in 'Series 3' and the traditional form but in contemporary English.

> Lamb of God, you take away the sins of the world: have mercy on us.
> Lamb of God, you take away the sins of the world: have mercy on us.
> Lamb of God, you take away the sins of the world: grant us peace.

Either version could be used either at the breaking of the bread or during the distribution.

Common Worship makes three small changes to the *ASB* provision. First, it provides an alternative text, 1 Corinthians 11.26, to 1 Corinthians 10.16–17.

> Every time we eat this bread
> and drink this cup,
> **We proclaim the Lord's death**
> **until he comes.**

This is less focused on the unity of the body of Christ and more on the Lord's broken body on the cross, perhaps with just a hint of the banquet of the Lamb at the end of time. Of course the Gospels avoid the word 'broken' in relation to the body of Jesus on the cross. Indeed John 19.33 makes the specific point that his legs were not broken by the soldiers, for he appeared already to be dead, but his side was pierced with a spear to make sure and out flowed blood and water. But this is to miss the point that the body of the Lord was 'broken' by torture and crucifixion; his whole body, not specific bones. And it was this body that had to be broken in that sense that brought salvation. So the bread of the Eucharist is broken so it may signify the broken body that redeems. For broken humanity, the identification of Christ with us in our humanity is a source of comfort and encouragement.

Second, *Common Worship* amends the *Agnus Dei* text, with 'sin' in place of 'sins' and bringing the two versions into line with one another, both now ending 'grant us peace'. There is a theological significance in the change from 'sin' to 'sins'. John 1.29, which is quoted here, uses the singular 'sin', though 1 John 2.2 uses the same phrase in the plural 'sins of the whole world'. The difference is that the singular implies, not the particular sins of individuals but the state of sin that afflicted the whole world and as a result cut us off from God. Previous versions opted to go with an understanding of the Lamb of God taking away an individual's sins, whereas the more modern versions focus more fully on the state of sin that affects the world.

Third, it gives stronger encouragement to use the *Agnus Dei* at this point in the liturgy: 'The *Agnus Dei* may be used as the bread is broken.' A note adds that 'sufficient bread for the whole congregation to share may be broken'. Individual wafers are thus discouraged because they make nonsense of the words 'We break this bread to share'.

In the end the breaking of the bread is an action, not a text, and on occasions it can be done in silence. But the texts from 1 Corinthians and the ancient song 'Lamb of God' draw out what is happening at this point in the liturgy. It is a profound theological moment.

18

The prayer of humble access

We do not presume
to come to this your table, merciful Lord,
trusting in our own righteousness,
but in your manifold and great mercies.
We are not worthy
so much as to gather up the crumbs under your table.
But you are the same Lord
whose nature is always to have mercy.
Grant us therefore, gracious Lord,
so to eat the flesh of your dear Son Jesus Christ
and to drink his blood,
that our sinful bodies may be made clean by his body
and our souls washed through his most precious blood,
and that we may evermore dwell in him, and he in us.

This prayer, long referred to as the 'prayer of humble access', though not so described in any of the rites, has been in use in every English rite since it was composed in 1548 and included it in the First English Prayer Book a year later. It has undergone minor changes of wording, has been challenged for its theological orthodoxy and has moved from place to place in the rite, but as a devotional prayer is much loved and committed by many to memory.

Archbishop Cranmer wrote it, drawing on a multitude of biblical and liturgical sources. His intention seems to have been to create for the laity an equivalent to the priest's private prayers before Communion in the Roman rite, essentially a prayer for worthy and fruitful reception of the sacrament. In 1549 he placed it as the very last words before the distribution, where the rubric states, 'Then shall the priest, turning him to

God's board, kneel down, and say in the name of all them, that shall receive the Communion, this prayer following'.

In 1552, where the order and the theology of the Eucharist have changed radically, the prayer has moved to the place that became familiar over the centuries, as a kind of interpolation in the Eucharistic Prayer, between the *Sanctus* and the prayer of consecration, the position it retained in 1662. We cannot know Cranmer's reason for moving it from the position for which he wrote it, though it is known that Bishop Stephen Gardiner had suggested that spoken after the consecration it implied adoration of Christ in his sacramental presence, something that Cranmer would by then have rejected. Its new position had less logic, which is no doubt why it was destined to move twice more.

The 1928 order moved the prayer to follow the penitential material that ended with the Comfortable Words. Thus it no longer interrupted the flow of the Eucharistic Prayer. 'Series 1' allowed it in either position, but a new rubric stated that 'the people may say it with him'. This was a legalizing of what had become common practice. In recent years it has become commonplace for it to be said together, even at a 1662 celebration, appropriately so, considering it was written as a devotion for the people. Presumably only a lack of literacy and familiarity made it, like some other prayers in the sixteenth-century rites, a prayer to be said by the priest alone.

'Series 2' made the use of the prayer optional, but went with the 1928 position after the Comfortable Words. However, this was beginning to seem less satisfactory, for now it became an intrusion between the prayers of penitence and the greeting of peace. More significant perhaps was the omission of the words 'that our sinful bodies may be made clean by his body, and our souls washed through his most precious blood'. An anxiety about these words had existed since soon after the 1662 book was authorized. Did they imply that it was the consecrated bread that cleansed only the body, but the consecrated wine that cleansed only the soul? That would not have been Cranmer's intention, but to reassure those who suspected inadequate theology, these lines were omitted. 'Series 3' modernized the language of the prayer, but made no other changes from 'Series 2'. *ASB* changed nothing.

The editors of *Common Worship*, however, unconvinced by the objections to the disputed lines, understanding them as poetic more than doctrinal, restored them. While this may be a fair interpretation, it is important to observe that the reference to our bodies being cleansed by Christ's body does not come from biblical tradition. It seems to be a conflation of the concept of being cleansed by his blood (which appears in the following line and which can be found in places such as 1 John 1.7 and Hebrews 9.13–14) with our bodies being cleansed by pure water (such as can be found in Hebrews 10.22). It is not entirely clear how Christ's body might effect cleansing. As a result, these two phrases must be read poetically and together if they are to make any theological sense.

Another odd, though very popular, feature of the theology of this prayer is the language of not being worthy to gather crumbs from under the table. This appears to be a conflation of two concepts: one of not being worthy in the presence of Christ and the other of gathering crumbs from under the table. The theme of being unworthy of Christ occurs in a number of places in the Gospel tradition. John the Baptist declared himself unworthy to carry Jesus' sandals (Matthew 3.11) and the centurion that he was unworthy for Jesus to enter his house (Matthew 8.8). Alongside these are Jesus' declaration of the necessity to take up our crosses to follow him if we are to be worthy of him (Matthew 10.38). But the reference to the crumbs under the table is surely alluding to the conversation between Jesus and the Syrophoenician woman (Mark 7.24–30), where the point is made that even dogs can eat those crumbs (the implication being that we do not need to be worthy to eat). This is one of those occasions when there is a conflation of allusions to being unworthy of Jesus, to the messianic banquet and to the Syrophoenician narrative; when taken together, these elements differ in meaning from their original use.

In terms of placing, *Common Worship* has not only put back Cranmer's words but also restored them to their original position. Removed from the position they occupied in all the rites from 1928 to 1980, they do not intrude in the *Common Worship* liturgy between the prayers and the Peace. Instead they become a response to the invitation, 'Draw near with faith', and a prayer for worthy reception immediately before the distribution.

In the devising of 'Series 3', the Liturgical Commission was of the view that people would not take kindly to a modernizing of the language of the prayer of humble access and that it would be preferable to produce a new contemporary prayer, with some of the same devotional feel as the old prayer, but with new imagery. The prayer was written by Professor David Frost and published in the report form debated by the General Synod. However, the Synod was not yet ready for such a radical change, rejected the new prayer and instead retained the old prayer of humble access in the new rite, editing it marginally to update the language. David Frost's prayer then disappeared from sight, but reappeared among the Appendices in *ASB*. *Common Worship*, recognizing it to be a fine text, but unlikely to be much used when hidden away in the Supplementary Texts, has brought it into the main rite as a clear alternative to the older prayer, though, like the other, an optional element in the rite.

Most merciful Lord,
your love compels us to come in.
Our hands were unclean,
our hearts were unprepared;
we were not fit
even to eat the crumbs under your table.
But you, Lord, are the God of our salvation,
and share your bread with sinners.
So cleanse and feed us

with the precious body and blood of your Son,
that he may live in us and we in him;
and that we, with the whole company of Christ,
may sit and eat in your kingdom.

As well as its biblical allusions, the prayer clearly owes something to George Herbert's poem, 'Love bade me welcome'. The inclusion of the idea of the insistent welcome offered by Love significantly changes the tone of the prayer. Although in many respects its theology is similar to the older prayer to which it is an alternative, the framing of the unworthiness of the supplicant by the insistent love of God changes the feel of the whole. The whole point of the Herbert poem was that while Love welcomed him in, it was his own sense of guilt and shame that prevented him from accepting. As a result, the emphasis of this prayer is now on the importance of laying down our feelings of unworthiness in order to accept the gracious invitation of God to share with him in the feast of the messianic wedding banquet, referred to in places like Matthew 22.

19

Words at the distribution

There are two sets of words to consider at the time of the distribution: first, those spoken by the president to invite people to Communion; second, those spoken by those distributing the consecrated bread and wine to each communicant in turn, although there is a significant overlap between the two.

There was no general invitation in Anglican rites until 1928, and it is helpful to begin with the words used to each communicant in the earlier rites. In 1549 the words used, reflecting the reformed Catholicism of that book, are

> The body of our Lord Jesus Christ, which was given for thee, preserve thy body and soul unto everlasting life.

> The blood of our Lord Jesus Christ, which was shed for thee, preserve thy body and soul unto everlasting life.

Very different are the words used in 1552, when a Protestant understanding of the sacrament has taken hold. There is no affirmation of the bread as body or the wine as blood. Instead the minister says, 'Take and eat this, in remembrance that Christ died for thee, and feed on him in thy heart by faith, with thanksgiving. Drink this in remembrance that Christ's blood was shed for thee, and be thankful.'

Faced with these two sets of words, representing very different understandings of the Eucharist, Elizabeth I's Prayer Book of 1559 combined them and 1662 followed in the same way. Thus the Catholic and Protestant formulations are brought together and both are spoken to each communicant.

In 1928 there was a recognition that this had created a very long text to be spoken to each person and that, with a large congregation, the distribution could take a very long time. So for the first time it proposed an invitation, using the two long texts woven into one, spoken to the entire congregation before anyone received, after which shorter sentences could be used for each communicant. This became established and forms part of all the succeeding rites, with very little textual variation, the form in *Common Worship* being

> Draw near with faith.
> Receive the body of our Lord Jesus Christ
> which he gave for you,
> and his blood which he shed for you.
> Eat and drink
> in remembrance that he died for you,
> and feed on him in your hearts
> by faith with thanksgiving.

In *ASB* the use of this text is mandatory. In *Common Worship* it is one of four options. Although as an invitation it only goes back to 1928, it is a classic Anglican text, expressing something important about the inclusive nature of Anglican eucharistic theology in the way that, since the sixteenth century, it has held two understandings together.

A second invitation in *Common Worship* is more directly biblical.

> Jesus is the Lamb of God
> who takes away the sin of the world.
> Blessed are those who are called to his supper.
> **Lord, I am not worthy to receive you,**
> **but only say the word, and I shall be healed.**

The first two lines pick up on John 1.29, where John the Baptist, seeing Jesus approaching, declares, 'Here is the Lamb of God who takes away the sin of the world.' The third line comes from Revelation 19.9: 'Blessed are those who are invited to the marriage supper of the Lamb.' It is, perhaps, a pity that the word 'marriage' has been omitted here since its inclusion would bring much more clearly to mind the messianic wedding banquet theme.

The congregational response is based on the words of the centurion who seeks the help of Jesus for his paralysed servant in Matthew 8.8: 'Lord, I am not worthy to have you come under my roof; but only speak the word, and my servant will be healed.' This text has been used in the Roman Mass since the sixteenth century, though there is an important Anglican textual variation. Whereas in the Roman rite the priest, holding up the host, says, '*This* is the Lamb of God', in *Common Worship* (as in *ASB* before it) the words are '*Jesus* is the Lamb of God' (emphasis added in each case).

The third invitation comes not from the Roman Mass but from the East, and is an early Greek text from the fourth century. In *ASB* it read: ·

> The gifts of God for the people of God.
> **Jesus Christ is holy,**
> **Jesus Christ is Lord,**
> **to the glory of God the Father.**

This was not a good translation. The most accurate translation of the Greek would be 'The holy things for the holy people.' The word 'gifts' was substituted for 'holy things' because that phrase seems unconvincing, but in doing so the relationship between the first line and the people's response has been lost. The invitation focuses the mind on what is holy: the things are holy and God's people are holy because God declares them to be so. But the congregational response notes that Jesus is the only one who is truly holy. *Common Worship* has rectified this.

> God's holy gifts
> for God's holy people.
> **Jesus Christ is holy,**
> **Jesus Christ is Lord,**
> **to the glory of God the Father.**

The final invitation is a seasonal one, for use for the 50 days from Easter Day to Pentecost. 1 Corinthians 5.7b–8 reads: 'For our paschal lamb, Christ, has been sacrificed. Therefore, let us celebrate the festival'. In *Common Worship*, with added 'alleluias', this becomes

> Alleluia. Christ our passover is sacrificed for us.
> **Therefore let us keep the feast. Alleluia.**

The only problem with this change is that changing 'paschal lamb' to 'Passover' moves the sense away from that which has been sacrificed to the feast in general. What is gained in sense by dropping the word 'paschal' is lost by the lack of clarity on Christ as the Passover lamb.

To return to the words used to each communicant, *Common Worship* has five sets, the first being a contemporary rendering of that classic Anglican set of words that has been in use since the reign of Elizabeth I. This is in contrast to what seems to have been the usage in the early centuries. The third-century *Apostolic Tradition of Hippolytus* says, 'The bread of heaven in Christ Jesus.' The fourth-century *Apostolic Constitutions* has simply, 'The body of Christ' and 'The blood of Christ, the cup of life.'

Common Worship allows, first, the economical 'The body of Christ' and 'The blood of Christ', which were given in 'Series 2' and return us to the *Apostolic Constitutions*. Second, it has the texts provided in 'Series 3', the slightly extended 'The body of Christ keep you in eternal life' and 'The blood of Christ keep you in eternal life', which reflect 1662's 'preserve thy body and soul unto everlasting life', but with an acknowledgement that eternal life begins in the here and now. Third, 'The body of Christ, broken for you' and 'The blood of Christ, shed for you', which also resonate with the 1662 version and its 'given for thee' and 'shed for thee'. The final set picks up on the *Apostolic Tradition* with 'The bread of heaven in Christ Jesus' and constructs, where the *Apostolic Tradition* gives no text for the consecrated wine, an equivalent set of words that owes something to the *Apostolic Constitutions*: 'The cup of life in Christ Jesus.'

Whichever words are used, in *Common Worship*, unlike the sixteenth- and seventeenth-century rites where the communicant receives in silence, the communicant says, 'Amen.'

20

Prayers after Communion

The Church gives thanks before sharing in the consecrated bread and wine. Indeed it is by giving thanks that the Church consecrates. So in a sense there is not much more to be said once Holy Communion has been shared, and it seems as if, in the early centuries, there were no further prayers. But as the liturgy became more formalized, prayers after Communion emerged, partly to recapitulate on the theme of the celebration, partly to express thanks for the gifts received and partly to pray that the sacramental grace received would make a difference in life beyond the liturgy.

In 1662, following 1552, there are two long and rich prayers provided for use after the distribution, but in those two liturgies there is little thanksgiving element before Communion. Instead they build into a crescendo of thanks and praise as the service reaches its climax in *Gloria in excelsis*. But that is not the way in contemporary rites, where the character of the post-Communion part of the service is to renew a sense of mission as the liturgy ends. *Common Worship* assumes a variable post-Communion prayer said by the president, a different prayer for each Sunday and feast day. It may be – and usually is – followed by a prayer said by the whole congregation. Two texts are provided in the main rite, four – one of which is a contemporary version of Cranmer's prayer of thanksgiving, which goes back to 1549 – in the Supplementary Texts.

The first such prayer in the main text is this.

Almighty God,
we thank you for feeding us
with the body and blood of your Son Jesus Christ.

114

Through him we offer you our souls and bodies
to be a living sacrifice.
Send us out
in the power of your Spirit
to live and work
to your praise and glory.

This prayer combines thanks for the feeding that has taken place with a continued offering of praise that will continue once the act of worship has come to an end. In terms of use of the Bible it is worth noting the addition of 'souls' into the wording of Romans 12.1–2. There it is simply our bodies (living, holy and acceptable to God) that are offered to God in response to his mercies, a phrase that contrasts sharply with the dead bodies offered in the sacrifice in the Temple. Intriguingly, in Romans 12.2 Paul moves on from bodies to talk about the transformation of our minds, but not of our souls. The closest reference to souls there is Paul's statement that handing over our bodies is our 'spiritual worship', as the NRSV translates it. Actually the Greek word used there is *logikos* and so the closest translation would be 'rational worship'. Nevertheless, although adding an extra concept into Romans 12, 'souls and bodies' implies the whole of our being and so seems a good formulation here.

This prayer has its origins in 'Series 2', though there it had no element of thanksgiving and attracted criticism for that and for the fact that people were to be sent out 'into the world' as if the Church were not part of the world. By the time of 'Series 3' it had taken on its present form, unchanged in *ASB* and *Common Worship*. There are echoes within it of the sixteenth-century texts.

The second prayer is another by Professor David Frost for 'Series 3'. Unlike his new prayer of humble access, it was not jettisoned by the General Synod, although it was amended. Designed originally as a presidential text, and given as such in

'Series 3' and *ASB*, it soon began to be used as a congregational prayer and, despite its theological complexity, has proved satisfactory said together. Like his other prayer, it draws richly on biblical and theological themes, in a dense and packed way, using resonant and beautiful language.

> **Father of all,**
> **we give you thanks and praise,**
> **that when we were still far off**
> **you met us in your Son and brought us home.**
> **Dying and living, he declared your love,**
> **gave us grace, and opened the gate of glory.**
> **May we who share Christ's body live his risen life;**
> **we who drink his cup bring life to others;**
> **we whom the Spirit lights give light to the world.**
> **Keep us firm in the hope you have set before us,**
> **so we and all your children shall be free,**
> **and the whole earth live to praise your name;**
> **through Christ our Lord.**

This prayer ranges from allusions to the prodigal son (Luke 15.20) concerning being brought home while we were still far off, to the Pauline incorporation into Christ through his dying and rising (Romans 6.4), and on again to Hebrews with the language of 'the hope set before us' (Hebrews 6.18). It is a pity that the General Synod altered David Frost's phrase 'Anchor us in this hope' to the weaker 'Keep us firm in the hope', losing the overt reference to Hebrews 6.19, 'We have the hope, a sure and steadfast anchor of the soul', though keeping the allusion to the previous verse (v. 18) about the hope that is set before us. It is also interesting to observe the fact that, in order to achieve three elements with three characteristics, 'the Spirit' is added to 'Christ's body' and 'his cup'. While living his risen life is an obvious characteristic of receiving his body, the other two – bringing life and light to others – are a less obvious outcome of receiving the cup and Spirit respectively, though they are a more general consequence of obeying the call to follow Christ.

Among the four prayers in the Supplementary Texts the most interesting and satisfying comes from the 1994 edition of the Church of Scotland's *Book of Common Order*. It reflects on the journey to Emmaus and the meal there recounted in Luke 24.13–35, though, in its ending, it has the worshipper engaging not only with the Jesus who is known in the breaking of bread, but also with the mystery of the Trinity.

> **You have opened to us the Scriptures, O Christ,**
> **and you have made yourself known in the breaking of**
> **the bread.**
> **Abide with us, we pray,**
> **that, blessed by your royal presence,**
> **we may walk with you**
> **all the days of our life,**
> **and at its end behold you**
> **in the glory of the eternal Trinity,**
> **one God for ever and ever.**

21

Blessing and dismissal

Although it may be argued that, after the blessing experienced in receiving the consecrated bread and wine of the Eucharist, no extra words of blessing at the conclusion of the service can add much to the service, a blessing by the president at the end of the liturgy had established itself before the eighth century. Thomas Cranmer did not challenge the convention and included in 1549 the text that has remained standard ever since. In its *Common Worship* form it is

> The peace of God,
> which passes all understanding,
> keep your hearts and minds
> in the knowledge and love of God,
> and of his Son Jesus Christ our Lord;
> and the blessing of God almighty,
> the Father, the Son, and the Holy Spirit,
> be among you and remain with you always.

It is based on Philippians 4.7, though the phrase 'the knowledge and love of God' is not part of the original text; instead it is borrowed from elsewhere in the Bible, such as Hosea 6.6.

The *Common Worship* Eucharist has a series of seasonal blessings, outside the compass of this book, and some other blessings for more general use. Some are drawn directly from Scripture:

> The God of all grace,
> who called you to his eternal glory in Christ Jesus,
> establish, strengthen and settle you in the faith;
> and the blessing . . .

> The God of hope fill you with all joy and peace in believing;
> and the blessing . . .

The first of these is 1 Peter 5.10 and the second Romans 15.13.
Ephesians 3.14–17 is the basis of this blessing:

> May the Father from whom every family
> in earth and heaven receives its name
> strengthen you with his Spirit in your inner being,
> so that Christ may dwell in your hearts by faith;
> and the blessing . . .

Others have resonances of Scripture, but are not direct quotations in the same way as those already mentioned.

> God the Father,
> by whose glory Christ was raised from the dead,
> strengthen you to walk with him in his risen life;
> and the blessing . . .

> Christ the good shepherd,
> who laid down his life for the sheep,
> draw you and all who hear his voice,
> to be one flock within one fold;
> and the blessing . . .

> Christ, who has nourished us with himself the living bread,
> make you one in praise and love,
> and raise you up on the last day;
> and the blessing . . .

> May God, who in Christ gives us a spring of water welling up to
>   eternal life,
> perfect in you the image of his glory;
> and the blessing . . .

Interestingly, of the formulations featured here, most are drawn
from John's Gospel. The first one (beginning 'God the Father')
has roots in Romans 6.4, but the other three are drawn from
John 10; 6.53; and 4.14 respectively, demonstrating how attrac-
tive John's imagery is to liturgical writers.

Although the blessing is, at least in theory, an optional part
of the liturgy, the words of dismissal are mandatory. This is

very different from 1549, 1552 and 1662, where the blessing is the last word. Words of dismissal give the whole of the last part of the service a different character, for they point to the truth that Christians are sent out from the Eucharist, nourished and renewed, to play their part in God's mission.

Since 'Series 2' a dismissal text has been the last word in the service. The precise text has changed more than once, but two forms are now well established.

> Go in peace to love and serve the Lord.
> **In the name of Christ. Amen.**

> Go in the peace of Christ.
> **Thanks be to God.**

The phrase 'to love and serve' may well be drawn from Deuteronomy 10.12, which exhorts the people of Israel to fear the Lord, walk in his ways, love him and serve him with all their heart and soul. Given that this is a dismissal, a reference to walking in the ways of the Lord might have been a helpful addition here. The alternative dismissal is less clearly drawn from a biblical text but contains hints of passages like Colossians 3.15 ('let the peace of Christ rule in your hearts').

The Latin dismissal in the Roman Mass is *Ite, missa est*, which means literally, 'Go, it is the dismissal' or 'Go, it is the sending.' The usual rendering in English of this text, 'Go, the Mass is ended', loses the sense of mission, of sending, which both the *Common Worship* texts express. They are brief imperatives, but highly significant if the Eucharist is to end on the right note.

In Eastertide the dismissal includes 'alleluias'.

> Go in the peace of Christ. Alleluia, alleluia.
> **Thanks be to God. Alleluia, alleluia.**

This is not the only point where 'Alleluia' features in the Eucharist. Every day, except in Lent, it may be used, better sung than said, to herald the Gospel. In Eastertide it is added to the sentence at the Peace. The Easter invitation to Communion uses it too. The word is from the Hebrew ('Praise Yah', 'Praise the Lord'). Cranmer used it in his Morning and Evening Prayer in English translation, 'Praise ye the Lord', and avoided the Hebrew, in the same way that he avoided 'Hosanna' (see Chapter 6). But contemporary liturgy has restored its frequent use as a word of joy, nearly always with paschal resonances. Its origins are in the Psalms and it is used also in Revelation 19.

The word 'Alleluia' (or in its more Hebraic form 'Hallelujah') is a word transliterated directly from Hebrew. The first part *hallelu* is the plural command, meaning 'praise', and the second part *jah* is a poetic abbreviation of the name Yahweh. Although the phrase occurs often in Psalms 111—117 and 145—150, the word 'Hallelujah' is not found in most Old Testament English translations because it is most often directly translated as 'Praise the Lord'. Like the word 'Hosanna', however, it was transliterated into Greek in the New Testament and, when it is, this is indicated by also transliterating it into English. In Christian usage the word has shifted slightly to be a word that is used to express praise, rather than being a command to praise. This is indicated in the liturgy by the way in which the congregation responds to the word 'Alleluia' with the same word.

As the last word of the Eucharist in Eastertide, it ensures that the liturgy finishes on a note of joy for those who have met the risen Lord in the breaking of bread.

Epilogue

One of the focuses of this book has been to identify those many occasions when the *Common Worship* eucharistic texts draw on the Bible and its theology. The eucharistic texts are a rich feast of theological ideas and allusions, but it can be all too easy to miss the depth and breadth of their references simply because we do not take time to reflect on the words being used and their significance. As we approach the end of the book, however, it is worth taking a small amount of time to reflect on what might be learnt from the way in which the Bible is used in the eucharistic texts.

Although direct quotations are used, probably the most common use of the Bible in these texts is through paraphrase or summary. Paraphrases or summaries of biblical narratives are particularly useful in the Eucharistic Prayers, where writers are attempting to communicate the whole sweep of salvation history in two or three lines. Take for example

> To the darkness Jesus came as your light.
> With signs of faith and words of hope
> he touched untouchables with love and washed the guilty clean

from Eucharistic Prayer D. These three lines allude to John's Gospel and its assertion that Jesus is the light of the world, to Jesus' miracles and teaching, to his method of healing (i.e. by touching people) and to his forgiveness of sins. Though the prayer does not contain direct quotations, it is relatively easy to identify, if not the actual passages that lie behind the text, the kind of passages that the author had in mind while writing the text.

This brings us to a particular interpretational decision that can commonly be found in liturgical texts. Although it is not always the case, liturgy more often than not opts for a harmonizing approach to Scripture. While it would have been possible, for example, to produce five different institution narratives for the Lord's Supper from the four Gospels and 1 Corinthians, in which each one drew exclusively from the aims and concerns of each Gospel/epistle, this approach has not been adopted; instead a single harmonized text has been achieved, often by omitting the unusual features present in each text. It is easy to see and even to defend why this has been adopted as an approach in the Lord's Supper, but there are other places within the liturgy where the original meaning of the passage has been altered as a result of the interpretational decision made.

This becomes particularly apparent when quotations or allusions are gathered from across a wide range of different books of the Bible. While not technically harmonization, the effect of placing texts together from a wide variety of original contexts provides the impression that the Bible is a monochrome text that is telling a single narrative from beginning to end, so that it is possible to place an allusion to Isaiah, to the Gospels, to Paul and to Hebrews next to each other and by doing so, evoke the Bible's view of a particular concept.

One of the major features of biblical scholarship over the past few centuries has been to insist on allowing the different strands of the Bible to stand as texts in their own right and to be read separately. The movement towards constant harmonization of narrative and ideas runs counter to biblical scholarship and as a result raises some important and interesting questions about the appropriate use of biblical texts.

These questions become particularly pressing when, within liturgy, allusions are made to biblical narratives. Does it matter if the effect of the allusion ends up being the opposite of what was clearly intended in the biblical narrative? We could answer this question in at least two ways. On the one hand we could argue that, since it is only allusion (i.e. a most general drawing of language or ideas), insisting on faithfulness to the text is nonsense. On the other hand we could argue that, since the

Bible is so clearly an important authority for liturgical writing, paying careful attention to its original meaning is vital.

Perhaps the best way to illustrate this is with the most obvious place where an apparent biblical allusion runs counter to the passage's original meaning. This occurs in the much beloved prayer of humble access where the members of the congregation declare that they are not worthy to gather up the crumbs from under the table. What has happened here is a conflation of the concept of being unworthy of Christ (for more on this see Chapter 18) and of the conversation between Jesus and the Syrophoenician woman in which she declared that even dogs could eat the crumbs from under the table. The point of the passage, though, is that although she was a Gentile, Jesus ended up recognizing that she *was* worthy to eat those crumbs (and hence receive healing for her daughter).

Is this a legitimate use of the Bible or not? Different people will give different answers to this question but it is worth being aware of the issues that it raises. It is entirely possible to be 'biblical' in alluding or even quoting from the Bible, while at the same time going against the grain of the passage in its original context. Most of the time the use of passages is not as extreme as this one, but nevertheless subtle shifts of meaning are achieved by putting together passages from different parts of the Bible. This technique has such a historic and honoured tradition that one wouldn't want to say that it *shouldn't* be done, but it is worth being aware of the issues and implications that arise when it *is* done.

The key thing is to be alert to the occasions when this happens and to reflect on a case-by-case basis on what this means about our use of Scripture, the meaning of the passage and the theology we espouse in worship. This book has not sought to answer all the questions that are raised by this approach but hopes to help readers to reflect for themselves on the theology that underpins what they say in worship week by week.

Another issue that arises is the choice of passages that lie behind the liturgical texts. Some passages are used again and again. Particular favourites are the parable of the prodigal son, the story of the Emmaus road and Romans 6.4. The language of John's Gospel is also often preferred to other language. In contrast, some books of the Bible are simply not used at all; for example there is little if any use of the great prophets Jeremiah and Ezekiel in the eucharistic texts, and equally very little of James from the New Testament. The effect of this is the forming of a liturgical canon within a canon, in which some texts from the Bible form the Christian mind through worship more than others do. While some might argue that the ministry of the word counterbalances this, the problem there is that so few churches today read or hear expounded the Old Testament – including the Psalms – that any counterbalancing remains at best partial.

Neither of these issues detracts from the majesty of the eucharistic texts that we pray week in, week out, but it is worth being aware that they raise questions that are worthy of further reflection as we seek to use the Bible in worship to the best of our ability.

* * *

The obvious response to a book such as this is that people have worshipped for years without a clear understanding of the theology that they are hearing, singing and saying, so why start now? Is it not, some might argue, the beauty and familiarity of the language that draws people to the heart of God and not a profound in-depth understanding of theology? An answer to such questions must surely be that people can, and do, worship using the eucharistic texts without any awareness of the theology they contain, but knowing a little about the history and theology that lies behind them can only aid our appreciation of them. It is a little like viewing a piece of art. It is perfectly possible to see a painting and to be transported by the beauty it contains, but a well-trained eye can help us appreciate the brush strokes, the light and darkness in the shading, and the perspective, which we might otherwise overlook.

This book has sought, both through an explanation of how the liturgical texts arrived in the form that they did and through reflections on the biblical resonances they contain, to draw people more fully into the majesty and beauty of the words of the eucharistic texts and ultimately, by doing so, enhance and enrich the experience of hearing, singing and saying these words week by week.

Index of biblical references

ND - #0055 - 270325 - C0 - 216/138/10 - PB - 9780281069132 - Matt Lamination